Pearl from the Orient

MADE IN HONG KONG

Pearl from the Orient
MADE IN HONG KONG

MARJORY BARNETT MILLER

Association of Baptists for World Evangelism
P.O. Box 8585
Harrisburg, PA 17105–8585
(717) 774–7000
abwe@abwe.org

ABWE Canada
160 Adelaide St. South, Suite 205
London, Ontario N5Z 3L1
(519) 690–1009
office@abwecanada.org

 PUBLISHING®

PEARL FROM THE ORIENT: Made In Hong Kong
Copyright © 2001 by ABWE Publishing
Harrisburg, Pennsylvania 17105

Library of Congress Cataloging-in Publications Data (application pending)

Miller, Marjory Barnett, 1935–
  Pearl From The Orient
  Autobiographical, Non-fiction
  ISBN 1-888796-27-8

Printed in the United States of America.

TABLE OF CONTENTS

Dedicated to Andrew and James,
my creative grandsons;
And to my students of the past 35 years
who have enriched my life.

FOREWORD

For most of my life, Marjory Barnett Miller has been like a little sister to me. When she returned from China, Mardie (as she was nicknamed) and I met for the first time. I was struck by her frail appearance. Mardie's young countenance reflected the trauma of her childhood experiences in the turbulence that was China in her formative years.

Locked inside her heart were stories that yearned to be told. Written at last, these vivid accounts are finally available to inform and inspire readers ready to enjoy a missionary adventure that unfolded in a remote land.

Mardie's parents, Rev. & Mrs. Victor Barnett, lived a colorful missionary life. They tasted suffering, endured hardship, and observed God's amazing grace breaking through into the lives of many people who had never before been exposed to the message of love, truth, forgiveness, and redemption in Christ.

Victor and Margaret Barnett pioneered ABWE's missionary work in China. God also used them to open Hong Kong as a new field for ABWE. When they retired to Grand Rapids, Michigan, in the 1960s, my wife, Sharon, and I were preparing to leave for our first term as new ABWE missionaries to Hong Kong.

The timing of their return from the field and our departure for that same field struck them and us as uniquely designed by the Lord to impress on us the sober responsibility of picking up the torch of gospel advance which they had carried with such valor for nearly 30 years. Sharon and I spent many hours in the Barnetts' home, learning all we could from this family who had been significantly used by God in the Chinese land and culture.

The legacy left by the Barnetts lives on in these pages. Mardie's fertile mind, vivid memory, and literary skills preserved and perpetuated the legacy upon which we continue to build even today—as missionaries, churches, and pastors in China faithfully exalt Christ and call people to saving faith.

This is not a book to speed-read. Take time to reflect on these adventures of faith. Pause to admire the valiant Chinese people who struggled under oppression and sought to survive the political intrigues of their time. Savor the joy of individuals discovering freedom in Christ. Rejoice in the birth of a church where none existed before. Weep with those who suffer persecution, with believers torn by conflict, with a nation sundered by war.

As you ponder the faith which endures, despite loss and deprivation, perhaps your own faith will be strengthened. Allow the Holy Spirit to move your heart in praise to the Good Shepherd who guides His sheep, even in the valley of the shadow of death. Respond to the Lover of your soul, as He stirs you to greater submission and sacrificial service.

May we be faithful to the Lord of the harvest in our generation, as the Barnetts were in theirs.

William Tracy Commons
ABWE Far East Administrator
May 2001

ACKNOWLEDGEMENTS

There are many people who made this book a reality, and it's impossible to name all of them. But I want to thank several of them who made significant contributions:

Dr. Dorothy Armstrong at Grand Valley State University, who first suggested that I write this book for the final two credits I needed for my master's degree;

"Grandma" Louise Cederlund, who took dictation as I began writing;

Barbara Ballast, who assumed the bulk of dictation responsibilities;

Donna Benedict, who typed the early drafts and hounded me to continue;

my son, David Miller, and Jamie Hawkins and Anita Swingle, all of whom proofread various drafts;

and Kristen Stagg at ABWE, who came across six handwritten chapters, encouraged me to complete the manuscript for publication, and then edited it.

one

MADE IN HONG KONG

Hong Kong is known as "The Pearl of the Orient." It was not always an inviting place. The British acquired the area from the Chinese in 1848 after the so-called "Opium War." The Treaty of Nanking, signed in 1842, states: "Victoria Island shall belong to England forever," while the other 390 square miles, including Kowloon and the New Territories, "shall return to Chinese possession in 1997."

The highest point in the British Crown Colony of Hong Kong is Victoria's Mountain, known among local English-speakers as "the Peak." Atop Victoria's Peak sits Matilda Hospital where I was born to Rev. Victor and Margaret Barnett, missionaries on the peninsula of Lui Chau, China, 250 miles southwest of Hong Kong. So you might say I was "made in Hong Kong."

My father, Victor Barnett, was born to the coachman of a manor house in Gloucestershire, England. In 1918 while serving with the Royal Air Force, my dad was sent to Egypt. But when the Boxer Rebellion broke out in China in the early 1900s, the British government decided its men were needed more in Asia, so Victor's RAF squadron was transported to Hong Kong. It took so long on the proverbial slow boat to China, however, that the turmoil was over by the time my father and his fellow airmen arrived.

In Hong Kong, Victor Barnett met Margaret Church, a young lady from Grand Rapids, Michigan. A missionary in western China under the Christian and Missionary Alliance mission board, Margaret had gone to Hong Kong for vacation after two years of studying the Mandarin language. When Margaret returned to the United States, Victor, after much difficulty, obtained a visa to travel there. He arrived in Boston, where the couple was married on July 21, 1930.

Soon the newlyweds returned to Hong Kong, where they heard of the need for missionary work in the Lui Chau Peninsula, the southernmost part of China. Five years later, Victor and Margaret Barnett were in Hong Kong, awaiting my birth.

My father told me that a year before I was born, a Christian man appeared in Lui Chau City. This unusual person had proven himself a great help in my parents' missionary work. Before leaving Lui Chau in January of 1935, the stranger told my parents that they would have a daughter before the year was over. Then he left, never to be heard from again. My father said he was "thrilled" with the news, as he wanted a daughter. He said, "I can teach a daughter to do boy things, but couldn't teach a boy to do girl things." Through the years my father and I worked closely together, and he did, indeed, teach me "boy things" which have helped me all my life.

The Peak is an enchanting place with its breathtakingly beautiful view of the South China Sea and coastline. The emerald green mountains, azure blue sea, and pearly white beaches are most inviting. All this can be seen from the cable car called the Peak Tram, which has been going up and down the mountain since 1885. At one point, the tram's incline is nearly vertical, laying passengers flat on their backs in the tram seats. It is said that in the old days, people liked to ride the Peak Tram in order to see the elderly Chinese men's queues (braids) sticking straight out at the steepest part.

Tropical gardens and shady walks surrounded Matilda Hospital, which offered its services to missionaries free of charge. Thanks to this policy, many MKs (missionary kids) were born there.

My birth on December 4, 1935, by Caesarean section, was

one of the first such deliveries in Hong Kong. Dr. Montgomery, a famous Australian, performed the procedure. My weight at birth was five pounds; a month later it had dropped to four pounds. I survived because of the special care provided by German nurses who sort of adopted me as "their baby." They even knitted and sewed my clothes. The Lord provided loving care at Matilda for three months.

The choice of an English name was significant for my parents. They named me Marjory (meaning "pearl"), after Marjory Mitchell, a Scottish lady who led my father to the Lord while he was stationed in Alexandria, Egypt, with the Royal Air Force. Jean, my middle name, came from Jean Johns, the Sunday school teacher who led my mother to the Lord at Wealthy Street Baptist Church in Grand Rapids, Michigan. The Chinese had given my parents the surname Baak, meaning "white." Since Marjory means pearl, some Chinese friends chose Mei Chu ("beautiful pearl") for my Chinese name. In China, the surname comes first, so I became Baak Mei Chu or White Beautiful Pearl. My name reminds me that God wanted me to be His "Pearl from the Orient."

During my three months in the hospital, my father stayed with an Australian businessman and his wife, Mr. and Mrs. Wilson. The Lord used the Wilsons to provide in many ways. Dr. Montgomery had said that I could be taken to my folks' remote station only if they owned a kerosene refrigerator, since there was no electricity in that remote spot. The Wilsons provided that refrigerator.

Another provision of the Lord was a Christian *amah* (nanny) named Di Goo. She traveled inland with my parents, not only to care for me, but also to become a Bible woman, serving the women of the local church. Di Goo later married Pastor Chen, whose wife had died, leaving him with nine children.

My first two years were spent in Lui Chau City, under the care of Di Goo and her nine step-children. My parents were busy in their mission work, which included translating the Gospels into the Lui Chau dialect. They had both learned the dialect during the five years before my birth under the tutelage of an elderly Chinese man who sat across the table from them and chanted the tones for them to acquire. This Chinese dialect was to be my first spoken language.

In the summer of 1938, my parents and I returned to the United States by way of England, in order to introduce me to my father's family. It would be almost 50 years before I saw Lui Chau City again.

KAI LING (CHICKEN HILL)

The complications of my birth were harbingers of things to come. At the age of three, I had completed my first trip around the world, although I remember almost nothing of it. A document, issued in Bristol, England, stated that," due to the ignorance of the law," I wasn't registered with the American Consul until I was two years old.

In actual fact, because I was one of the first Caesarean deliveries in Hong Kong and had such a low birth weight, my survival was uncertain. By the time everyone realized I would make it, no one thought of registering me except with the British government, which later caused some difficulty.

I knew of an American family who had a baby while traveling on a German ship. When they reached a port, the family was allowed to disembark but the baby could not because he was not registered as an American citizen; he was considered a German citizen. The family was held up with legal knots that took some time to untangle.

One unusual and near-fatal incident occurred when I was three, traveling on a German freighter from the United States to Shanghai. A four-year-old boy rode his tricycle around the deck, with me standing on the back of it. It was great fun! Until a huge gush of water flooded the deck, and we went sailing toward the edge. Just before we were swept overboard, a sailor grabbed us. That flood of water came from the upper deck, where someone decided to empty the swimming pool. God kept us from taking a swim—of the permanent kind—in the Pacific Ocean.

When my family arrived in Hong Kong, my folks learned they could no longer return to Lui Chau City because communist activity already threatened lives in that area. Mom and Dad decided to go to a town called Chek Hom, 10 miles inland from the French seaport of Fort Bayard, where our friends, the Jay Morgan family, were missionaries. This whole area, including Chek Hom, was part of French Indochina until 1946.

My parents and I were the first missionary family to live in Chek Hom. Our home consisted of several rooms above the storefront church. I celebrated my fourth birthday in my father's garden on the flat roof, a typical location for the Chinese to keep their gardens of potted flowers.

Chinese New Year of 1939 was great! Our verandah (porch) provided us with front-row seats for the parade. An enormous, slithering dragon, held aloft by men carrying poles and running along under the giant puppet, was a main feature. The only thing that I found scary was the 20-foot string of firecrackers set off across the street when the dragon drew near. The man under the dragon head had to climb on the shoulders of four people, one on top of the other, to reach the sack of good luck money at the top. The money was at the end of a long string of lighted firecrackers, and he had to reach the money before the biggest firecracker at the very top exploded and shook all the surrounding buildings.

By 1940, my father acquired land on a hill outside of Chek Hom, known as Kai Ling (Chicken Hill). It commanded a beautiful view of Chek Hom and an arm of the South China Sea. Mother used to quote Rudyard Kipling's poem: ". . . when the sun comes up like thunder, out of China 'cross the bay. . . ." We often stopped to admire the beautiful sunrise from our verandah.

Our compound, a walled area which included the house,

garden, and servants' quarters, was built in 1940. As the walls went up, my father and I slept on grass mats at night to guard the bricks. At four years of age, I learned how to lay bricks. It was so exciting to help plan the garden—where to lay the cement walks, what kinds of trees to plant.

When the compound wall was finished and the big gates at the top and the small gates at the bottom were in place, the three of us moved in. I had my own room that opened out onto the verandah. The living room took up the middle one-third of our house and had French doors at either end that opened onto the front and back gardens.

The Kai Ling house even had running water, a flush toilet, a sink, and a ceramic-tiled bathtub shipped in from Hong Kong. Water cisterns to catch rainwater were built at each end of the verandah. Four other cisterns, connected by pipes in the ground, were spaced down the hill in our compound to hold the over-flow. This ensured our water supply through the dry season. Heating tap water wasn't necessary; the hot weather took care of that job for us. Boiled water to wash dishes was heated on the kerosene stove after we cooked our meal.

We actually welcomed a cold bath because of the unrelent-ing tropical heat. In fact, if we stopped the drain in the tub overnight, moisture condensation from the ceramic tile wall filled the tub with plenty of water. Because we lived only 20 degrees north of the equator, on a level with Mexico City, tem-peratures averaged 90° or more, with equal amounts of humidity.

Our garden became a symbol of peace. Mother made up a game we played during a full moon. She blindfolded me and led me down the garden path. Then, removing the blindfold, I had to identify the shadow of the plant on the sidewalk at my feet. Mother even wrote a poem about our beautiful garden:

IN MY GARDEN

Oh my Kai Ling garden fair,
In the spring I would be there.
When the blossoms, fragrant, reign,
Drift against my windowpane.
When at dawn, cicada's song
Drowns the booming temple gong.
Oh my Kai Ling garden fair,
In the spring, I would be there.

When the heavy golden moon
Rises from the far lagoon,
On the garden path I see
Lovely lacy imagery.
And the passing breezes beat
Leafy lyres for fairy feet.
Oh my Kai Ling garden fair,
In the eve I would be there.

Summer rosy rainflowers grow,
When the rainbow arches low.
Autumn's flowers celosia bloom,
Red and wine and golden plume.
Bougainvillea o'er the wall,
Lets its purple glory fall.
Oh my Kai Ling garden fair,
There shall be no winter there.

t h r e e

CHINESE SCHOOL

After my parents established our home on Kai Ling, it was time to think about starting my schooling. Although my first language was the Lui Chau dialect, we now lived farther north where the language was Cantonese, so that became my new main language. On Chicken Hill, our neighbors were two Chinese families: two young couples with two small children each. I enjoyed playing with the children, and they helped me acquire the Cantonese language.

My mother decided to start teaching me how to read English. Since we spoke Cantonese at home, she had to explain everything in Chinese. She began with the alphabet and the phonetic sounds each letter made. It seemed hopeless to me, and the frequent interruptions made us both decide to give up the attempt. Instead, I would attend Chinese school.

You may wonder what interruptions cancelled those early attempts at English lessons. On one occasion, our neighbor, Mrs. Li, was caught stealing vegetables in another village. She stood outside our compound wall, crying for help, and holding her partly cut-off ear in her hand. Mother had to clean it; put the ear back on the best she could; and bandage Mrs. Li. Then the wound needed to be tended every day for several weeks.

Another time, the other young mother on our hilltop did not get up, and her husband came to ask for help. Mom crawled into their mud hut and found the woman unconscious. Mom bathed and cared for her, but the young mother eventually died. The family came from a faraway village, so the Chinese church members made the wooden casket and sewed the new outfit in which the woman would be buried. She was the first person I helped prepare for burial.

The local church gave her a Christian burial, for which her husband was extremely grateful. I remember him kneeling down and expressing his heartfelt thanks for all their kindness. It was different from the typical Chinese funeral with paid mourners and long, drawn-out rituals.

Attending Chinese school meant being taken down Chicken Hill and through the village to a privately owned school. Kindergarten lasted for two years. The first year was half days and the second year was full days, six days a week, as well as reporting to school for flag-raising on Sunday.

By the time first grade came around, I was six, going on seven, old enough to take a shortcut through two villages on my own. One day my father accompanied me. A group of around 20 children chanted, "Foreign devil! Foreign devil!"

Father stopped and explained that we were the same as they; only our skin was a different color. I had never before thought of the fact that I was different, maybe because I had no accent; Chinese was my native language. Father explained that we lived in China in order to tell them that Jesus loved them.

The next time Father accompanied me through that village, about 50 children ran along chanting, "Here comes the Jesus man." Some of these same children attended our church school after the war, and grew up to become leaders in the local church.

First grade was hard work. School started at 7 a.m. and lasted until 4 p.m. Morning recess was spent raising the flag and singing the national anthem. Afternoon recess was reserved for planned calisthenics. We had half an hour to eat the lunch we brought from home.

A few rich students had hot dinners brought in by their servants. Those meals consisted of vegetables, hot steaming rice, and an ancient egg (which most people would call a rotten egg). The aroma was something to run away from: an unforgettable, unappetizing odor. I was never brave enough to get past the smell to taste one.

In the classroom, all of us students sat on backless benches and worked at benches that were a little higher. We had to bring our own rice-paper copy books, reading books, a stick of ink and a dish in which to grind the ink, a camel's-hair brush for writing Chinese characters, and slate and chalk for math. We also used an abacus to work math problems.

In China, educated people are highly respected. Immense respect is expected to be given to a teacher. Students talking out of turn was an unthinkable breach of etiquette. When the teacher entered the classroom to start class, a designated student would say, *"Yat"* (one). At this cue, the class stood. At the signal *"Yi"* (two) all of us bowed. *"Saam"* (three) was the cue for all of us to be seated. We also stood to answer when the teacher called our names.

One morning, our teacher discovered that someone had made a mark on the whitewashed outhouse wall. Since no one confessed, the teacher lined up the entire schoolroom and used his ruler to rap smartly on the palm of each student's hand. We all went home with blisters that day.

Chinese is a tonal language. A different tone for the same sound could mean something very different. *Tong* with a rising or falling inflection means, among other things, "Chinese," "candy," "to iron," "to kill," or "soup." Chinese uses characters instead of an alphabet. Each character conveys a complete idea and has only one syllable. A student needs to be able to recognize over 3,000 characters before he can read a simple novel.

In order to pass first grade, I had to be able to read the Chinese newspaper and recite the addition, subtraction, multiplication, and division tables forward and backward. We learned them as a chant. Maybe the fact that we recited numbers and reading lessons aloud together is the reason we were too tired to talk. Plus, after walking a mile to school, it was almost easy to sit still!

After the long walk home, I had chores to do and at least two hours of homework to complete by the light of a kerosene lamp. If homework was not finished on time, a student could expect the ruler to be applied in accordance with the amount of work not completed. All of us quickly learned that homework completed on time was preferable to painful blisters.

School was not all hard work. Because art is a great part of Chinese culture, we often sang and put on plays. Sometimes we took daylong hikes. My mother baked banana bread, made from bananas we grew in our yard, to take along for my lunch. (To this day, banana bread is still one of my favorite foods.) During the hike, we stopped to get cool drinks of water from springs along the path.

Although life consisted of hard work, even for a child as young as I was, in many ways it was good training for the days that lay in the not-too-distant future.

f o u r

THE WAR YEARS

The storm clouds of World War II rolled in, bringing thousands of refugees from northern China who were trying to escape the Japanese. My parents and I lived at the southern tip of China, the jumping-off point to Hainan Island and adjacent to French Indochina (now called Vietnam). Because the French controlled our part of the country and France had not yet fallen to Germany, we were still free.

Then, one Sunday as we left church in downtown Chek Hom and were walking toward the main street, we saw the Japanese Army marching through town. At the head were the officers riding huge horses, followed by tanks and other war machines. When they saw my parents and me, some of the soldiers rushed down the side street toward us.

But the Lord had a hiding place ready for us. The family of one of my classmates owned a rice shop right at that spot. My friend's father grabbed us and hid us behind the rice urns. The store was closed, so when the soldiers got there, we were nowhere to be seen. They rejoined their parading army.

A few Sundays later when my parents and I returned to our compound after church in Chek Hom City, the French vice-governor was there to meet us. He explained, through an interpreter, that our freedom would be curtailed. My father and fellow missionary Uncle Jay Morgan, from Fort Bayard, were to be taken into custody overnight. The Morgans, an American family, lived only 10 miles from us. Jaymes, two years older than I, was a great playmate of mine; Ann Morgan's birth in 1942 had been an occasion for excitement all around.

Life grew ever harder in our part of China. I will never forget the look on my father's face on the morning of December 8,
1941 (which is December 7 on the other side of the International Date Line). After he had secretly listened to the short-
wave radio, hidden beneath the floor tiles under his bed, Father
left the house in a hurry, taking all the money we had. He used
it to purchase rice and a five-pound can of Klim ("milk" spelled
backwards, a brand name for British powdered milk). He also
told his banker friend and the manager of the hotel what he had
heard on the radio, and they, too, bought all the rice they could.

Within 20 minutes, news of Pearl Harbor reached our part
of China and the bottom dropped out of the local currency. A
loaf of bread went from $5 to $500 and, by night, paper money
was of no value at all. Later that week, several tons of bundled
paper money were burned in a huge hole on Kai Ling.

From then on, we ate one meal a day with gratefulness to the
Lord. We had a strange diet, but the Lord's presence showed in
His provision and protection.

Immediately after the Pearl Harbor incident, my family and
the Morgans were put under "house arrest," but ordered to carry
on church services as usual so that the general population would
not be disturbed by this new turn of events. Our services were
strictly monitored by Japanese informants, as was every movement we made.

But now we were in the midst of war. Bombings became an
almost daily occurrence. Father sent Mother and me 20 miles
away to spend Christmas with the Chen family. Their village was
located in a dense forest, which hid them from the Japanese
planes. Mrs. Chen (Di Goo, as I called her) had been my *amah* in
Lui Chau City when I was a baby.

Mother and I started the 12-hour trip by wheelbarrow car-
avan at 4 a.m. The wheelbarrow had a seat on each side of the
wheel, where Mother and I sat holding umbrellas to shield our-

selves from the hot sun. Some wheelbarrows transported passengers while others held cargo; each wheel emitted a different—but equally annoying—squeak.

The Chens said, "We heard you coming long before you arrived, so we knew when to leave our house in the ox cart to pick you up." They were a welcome sight to Mother and me after hours of traveling in the heat over rough land dotted with wild pineapples.

The Chens' home was typical of most Chinese homes at that time, rectangular in shape, with the rooms built around a courtyard. There, in the courtyard under the trees, they cooked, ate, washed clothes, ironed, and, yes, bathed in a large wooden tub. After the dusty hot trip, a tub bath felt good.

Even the bed made of boards afforded Mother and me a good night's sleep, despite the fact that chickens and ducks also shared the "family room" (courtyard). A moon gate, which is a round doorway with a sill two feet off the ground, kept the animals from escaping the courtyard. And so, Christmas of 1941 was a blessed time of peace and joy that the outside world could not have given us.

Some of the refugees who reached us in Chek Hom had been wealthy, used to extravagant living. They had difficulty eating the small, brown eggs of the local pullets when they were accustomed to large, white eggs.

At that time, my parents owned about 16 hens and a rooster. The wealthy refugees were willing to pay well for a dozen leghorn eggs to set, in order to hatch their own chickens. This business venture kept us supplied with enough money to buy one meal a day for six months—until the night we heard noise in the hen house.

Father shone his foot-long flashlight down the walk just in time to see a thief jump the compound's six-foot wall. I remember my father and mother saying, "Guess we were depending more on the chickens than on God!" With the theft of our rooster, we were out of the egg business.

Then a typhoon hit. The typical pattern for these storms is strong winds blowing from one direction, followed by a half-hour calm during which rain pours down in torrents. Then the strong winds blow from the opposite direction. During the lull in this typhoon, we shored up everything we could in preparation for the strong backlash winds, which is when trees and walls topple over.

It was during the calm that one of the Christians from the downtown church in Chek Hom reported that the South China Bible College and their staff of around 20 foreigners had arrived at the church. The students bedded down, wall-to-wall, at the church. The missionaries—Americans and Canadians—moved into our house, and our living room became their dorm. They stayed for several weeks until my father could figure out a way to smuggle them past the Japanese-controlled border into free China.

All this time, God provided enough food for one meal a day for the entire group. Our meal was made from wheat that took my father over an hour to grind between two large stones. The fine flour was used to make pancakes; the coarser part was cooked on a charcoal stove. Then we boiled six-inch slabs of molasses from the Chens' village. After the molasses was boiled and the bees, flies, straw, and sand had been strained out, it was fit to eat and delicious. Soybeans ground with water formed a white liquid. We were all set: pancakes with syrup one day, and cereal with soy "milk" and molasses the next.

Our unexpected guests soon learned to enjoy the daily feast. At suppertime we gathered in shifts around the kitchen table to thank the Lord for protection and meeting our needs, even though there was no food to eat since we'd already had our daily meal.

One day our hotel manager friend sent up enough peanuts for three apiece. Dr. Oldfield, a practical joker, sat next to me. He told me to look at a picture on the wall. As I looked where he pointed, he swiped my three peanuts and ate them. That was one joke he wished he had never pulled! Mother calmly told him there were no more peanuts. I loved Dr. Oldfield, even if he did snitch my food. I used to sit on his knee while he told about his many years in China.

One such story I recall involved Dr. Oldfield's escape from certain death. Back in the 1920s, communist bandits put a price on Dr. Oldfield's head. He was tired of their threats, so he set off on foot over the mountains to find the bandits. When he finally located them, he said, "I hear you are looking for Pastor Paau (Dr. Oldfield's Chinese name). I know where he is. Follow me!"

He led them all over the mountains until, one by one, they wore out and gave up. He went home and was never bothered by them again. They never knew that Dr. Oldfield was Pastor Paau, the man they were hunting.

Our lives on Kai Ling went on in spite of the bombings. One morning in Chinese school, we children went to the stadium about a half mile from school to practice marching. We were given a few minutes to swing. While I was swinging, a plane seemed to come from nowhere. There was no time even to sound the air-raid warning. The bombs dropped just on the other side of the ball field.

I had a front-row seat! I could not get the swing to slow down enough to jump off, so I watched the bombs dropping all around me. It turned out to be one of the safest spots. By the time I got off the swing, the plane was gone. I ran back through the village to my school, only to find the windows blown out. We swept up the glass and continued school as usual.

On another occasion, I happened to mention to my folks that my seatmate was not in school because she had smallpox. We usually were inoculated each year, but because of the war, no medical supplies were available. My folks contacted a refugee nurse friend who had some serum, and I got the smallpox vaccine.

A week later, I was covered with more than 50 of what looked like smallpox lesions. The odd part was, I wasn't sick. Then the nurse discovered that I had scratched the vaccination while scratching my mosquito bites, and re-inoculated myself all over my body. I guess I vaccinated myself for life because after that experience, I never had a smallpox vaccination that "took." After my last inoculation in 1960, Dr. Roth said, "No take, no charge."

Another time I said, "Chung Lao won't be returning to school because he died of cholera." In the past, news like this prompted my mother to buy serum and, with her Chinese helpers, give injections to hundreds of Chinese whenever a plague broke out in a nearby village. On those occasions, it was my job to keep a charcoal fire going under the boiling water used to sterilize the needles. During the war, however, there was no serum, so nothing could be done but trust the Lord. Many who had not been inoculated died during this cholera epidemic.

I can remember during epidemics that dying people clung to our compound wall, screaming for help, before they died about 20 minutes later. It was my father's job to bury the dead because no Chinese person would get near contaminated corpses. The stench of death is unforgettably horrifying.

Missionary work is not just preaching. My parents were always ready to serve, no matter what the need. When a fire broke out one night in a settlement of mud huts across the road, the fire department was, of course, summoned. But meanwhile, the fire had to be contained. If it crossed the road, another 60,000 mud huts, our compound, and everything else would go up in smoke.

Water was scarce, but one thing every family had was a large urn of urine used on the vegetable gardens. Being creative (or, more likely, inspired by God) Father made use of the urine to keep the fire from jumping the road and destroying more than the small village. We heard the ding-ding of the fire engines (wheelbarrows with barrels of water) being pushed up the hill. They arrived just in time—the fire was out!

Above:
Matilda Hospital where Marjory was born

Below:
Victor and Margaret Barnett with baby Marjory,
Lui Chau City, 1936

arjory at 6 months old; wearing shoes
nd made by Di Goo, in Lui Chau City

usins in England, 1937

Map of South China

Above:
Marjory and her cycling playmate aboard a German ship

Below:
Barnett house in Chek Hom

Above:
Victor Barnett (right) with Chung Sau in front of the tower his grandfather built, 1938

Below:
Victor Barnett and Jaymes Morgan, Sr.

Marjory and Margaret Barnett exiting a tonga in India, 1944

...ake Surprise, where Victor Barnett baptized many ...hinese believers

Titus and Marjory, fledgling builders, 1947

Margaret Barnett in front of a bombed-out building in Manila

...ragon parade to celebrate the Chinese New Year

...eaches around the Pacific were littered with the remains of sunken ships from World War II.

Hong Kong's Peak Tram

Below:
School lessons in Chek Hom garden

Victor, Margaret, and Marjory (age 3) Barnett
in Michigan

Marjory, age 10, and Chee Kwun, lifelong
friends

During the war, the ubiquitous Japanese could be identified by their inability to speak Chinese. Without my parents' knowledge, I made a deal with some enemy troops: if they would give my friends and me a ride part-way to school in their truck (thereby saving us the walk to school past the house of the "crazy lady" in the village), I would teach them English. The funny part about this is that I knew only a few words of English myself. The deal worked fine until Father found out. Then it was back to walking to school through the stinky villages and past the "crazy lady's" house.

One Sunday after church, Mother and I were walking up the hill toward our walled compound when a small, pretty young lady followed us, speaking a strange language and wearing several hats. I had heard that the "crazy lady" dressed like this. Could this be her? As we neared our gate, it was obvious that the "crazy lady" planned to enter behind us.

It was then that Mother discerned the problem. She said, "That's not a crazy lady. She's possessed by a demon." Mother prayed for wisdom, then spoke in English, commanding the demon not to come any closer. To my surprise, the Chinese woman answered Mother in English. Then Mother spoke in French, then the Lui Chau dialect, and finally Mandarin. Each time, the young lady answered in that language.

We closed the doors and barred the gate with a 4 x 4, before rolling a two-foot-thick concrete cylinder against the door. Even with all this, when the possessed woman pushed with her hand, the door almost caved in. Mother commanded her in Christ's name to leave. We did not see her again until the day she appeared to tell us she'd been delivered from demons. She was a beautiful young woman, able to speak only Cantonese.

One blessing of the war years was that we often spent the evenings outside because of the bombing. The American Air Force stationed at Kueilin paid periodic visits to drop bombs on our area. We set up our cots and mosquito nets, and camped out.

My mother enjoyed studying astronomy, so she taught me how to identify planets and constellations. I remember how excited she was to see the Southern Cross. The view of the night sky from our hill was hard to describe. With no electric lights to interfere, it was like seeing diamonds glisten against black velvet.

Another blessing of those uncertain times was the new friends God gave us among the refugees. Some such friends were the Lo, Wong, and So families. The Lo (pronounced "Law") family included a son, Wing Lok, and a daughter, Chee Kwun, around my age. For a while they lived in buildings at the foot of our compound. Chee Kwun and I wore the same size and shared our clothes.

On my eighth birthday, Mother and Mrs. Lo planned a surprise party. Father took about 10 of us on a hike to some canyons beyond the next hill, which boasted the only high school in the area. A small canyon that had a grassy slope was the quickest way down the hill. We started at the top and rolled all the way down into a sandy-bottomed creek that was about two-feet deep. By the time we climbed back to the top, the tropical sun had dried us completely and we were ready for another roll. When we arrived home around 5 p.m., Mother and Mrs. Lo had a surprise garden party.

Around this time, Father and Uncle Jay Morgan rode on their bicycles to an outstation called Awn Po, where they had rented a storefront to hold meetings. My father, being "chief cook and bottle washer," went to the market at 4 a.m. It was first come, first served for the freshest meats and vegetables.

With their meal on the table ready to be eaten, Father and Uncle Jay heard the air-raid siren go off. After all that work, they were not about to miss a good meal, so they started to eat. Then, rice bowls still in hand, they landed under the table when a bomb blew up the medicine shop across the street. They got plenty of home remedies added to their meal!

Digging out their bikes, the pair headed for the park down

the road. But before they reached safety, the planes returned for another strafing. The two men missed the spray of bullets by lying in a ditch. After that close call, Father and Uncle Jay decided to head home, a 20-mile ride from Awn Po. On reaching a cross-roads, the missionaries were told by some Chinese peasants that the Japanese army was advancing right behind them. They pedaled faster than they ever had in their lives, and made it home before the Japanese regiment arrived. The Lord gave them the strength to "beat" an army.

five

MIDNIGHT ESCAPE AND
A SURPRISING RESCUE

On December 20, 1943, two weeks after my eighth birthday, Father and Uncle Jay Morgan were summoned again for an audience with the French vice-governor. This time the news was worse: France had fallen to Germany. The Japanese, Germany's allies, decided they were in charge.

The vice-governor advised the foreigners, "It is time for you to leave." He was interested in them reporting the situation to ouside help, who might be able to evacuate the French families. But how could the two missionary families escape? Much prayer went into our decision. Preparation for a long, overland journey across China was a huge task. Travel money had to be raised by selling off what little remained of our possessions, and we needed to prepare dried food to take with us.

New Year's Eve found us all in the downtown church in Chek Hom. The Christians planned a Chinese dinner, which we used as a cover-up for our escape. Our party consisted of the Morgans—Uncle Jay, Aunt Dorothy, Jaymes, age 10, and Ann, age one that very day—Father, Mother, and me.

Around 4 a.m. on January 1, 1944, we left through the back alley with Chinese Christians to guide us. After an hour's walk in the dark with flashlights, we reached the arm of the South China Sea, which we had to cross in order to reach free China.

Immediately, we faced what seemed to be insurmountable obstacles. A reinforced concrete tower with Japanese sentries on guard to prevent any attempts to escape to free China stood between us and the hired junk, a large Chinese sailboat. The tide was out, which meant one-eighth of a mile of mud separated us from our boat. Father bargained with Chinese coolies—men who carried heavy burdens—to carry us piggyback out to the junk. When that was settled, we were ready to sneak past the sentinels before sunrise. As we reached the tower, we found them all asleep, much to our great surprise and equally great relief. Even the guard at the front entrance slumped over his machine gun. The Lord had put them all to sleep.

We were quite a sight! One man carried Jaymes and me in his arms, while the four adults each rode on the back of a coolie. Ann was carried out to the boat by her *amah*. We reached the junk safely under cover of darkness. As dawn broke over the South China Sea, there was no wind to fill the sails of our boat. There we sat, like the proverbial ducks. The only thing to do was to pray, which we did down inside the boat.

As we prayed, we heard a boat motor. How could that be? The vice-governor owned the only motorboat in the area, but the Japanese had confiscated it. Had they discovered our escape attempt? Why was a motorboat riding in that area at that time of the morning? What should we do? Just then a voice shouted, "Any foreign devils on board?"

It did not take long for my father to recognize what he needed to do. He climbed up on deck, waved his white helmet, and called, "Here we are!"

The motorboat drew close to reveal the French vice-governor himself. He waved his own white helmet and called back, *"Bon voyage!"* He had been anxious to know that we got away safely.

As the vice-governor's motorboat left, God sent the wind which took us safely to the unoccupied coast of free China.

It was a great relief to have reached free China, though Burma, India, the mined waters of the Indian Ocean, and the thick of the battle in the South Pacific theatre still lay ahead of us. We would experience 10 months of difficult travel before my parents and I really would be free in the "good ol' USA."

The first order of business upon arriving in free China was to hire coolies and sedan chairs for the next eight days of travel. We and the Morgans spent our first night in a bombed-out marketplace. The village was now occupied by Nationalist troops sent in to hold back the advancing Japanese. As we traveled, we remained only one step ahead of them each day. Jaymes and I found a bomb crater big enough to lay our one blanket in; it made a good bed.

All of a sudden, Uncle Jay asked, "What's for supper? Where's our New Year's feast?" Aunt Dorothy had a ready answer, producing a cake baked in a saucepan, complete with one candle to celebrate Ann's first birthday. Aunt Dorothy had saved the flour, painstakingly sifting out all the little critters. Ann will never have another birthday cake like that first one.

The next day we started out in four sedan chairs. A sedan chair is a wicker box suspended from shoulder poles carried by two people who use a peculiar, bouncing gait as they tread the narrow paths. Thank the Lord that they were surefooted! Mother and Aunt Dorothy each had a sedan chair. Father and Uncle Jay traded the use of another one, taking turns walking. Jaymes and I shared one, much to the distress of the coolies. Every time we had a tug-of-war over the blanket, the coolies set the chair down. It seemed our wiggling caused them shoulder pain.

There were no roads to follow through the countryside covered with tall grass and wild pineapples. The occasional mud huts and a clump of trees provided a spot where everyone rested in the shade from the sub-tropical sun. During one of these rest periods, Aunt Dorothy brought out homemade peanut brittle. *Ho ho sik!* (Good, good, eat!)

Sometimes the terrain was too steep for the couriers to carry the chairs. At such times, we all got out and walked. One day,

Aunt Dorothy handed baby Ann to my father so she could get out of the chair. She warned, "Watch out. Ann is wet." During the war, there were no rubber pants, and only old towels for diapers.

With outstretched arms, my father took Ann, stepped back into the tall grass—and disappeared! At Aunt Dorothy's screams, the rest of us came running. We found my father wedged down in an abandoned well. Because his ams were outstretched, holding the baby, he had stuck only partway down the narrow well.

He yelled, "Please get me out!"

Uncle Jay asked, "Vic, what are you doing down there?"

My father responded, "Never mind! Just please get me out!"

We didn't even have a rope with us. The coolies formed a human chain to reach my father. He climbed out with only a few scrapes and bruises. We were all grateful to the Lord for His protective care of Ann and my father. After they were safely rescued, we investigated the well. We estimated it was approximately 40 feet deep.

Little Ann thought the whole episode was quite a lark, arranged just for her benefit. She was happy and laughing throughout. Years later in Japan, Ann won a writing contest with her composition entitled "How I Saved a Man's Life at the Age of One."

Each day of our trek brought its challenges. We stayed overnight in Chinese hotels. A "hotel room" in such a place had board beds with grass mats on top; a Chinese meal was provided, too. We woke one morning to find all our coolies were gone, our baggage with them. No one knew what had happened to them. But we had to keep moving in order to stay ahead of the advancing Japanese, who now occupied the villages we had just left.

The next night we stayed in a brick hotel with a flat rooftop. We went up on the roof to cool off. I had Ann by the hand as we walked in the roof garden. All at once, she took a step by herself. She was such a joy to us all. And what a welcome diversion from the desperateness of our situation!

As we traveled village to village, we woke one morning to find that our missing coolies and all our baggage had reappeared. One of the coolies had learned of a relative's wedding in another village, and the whole group decided to attend the festivities without letting anyone know.

The days went by with many surprises and evidences of God's care. We finally reached Liu Chow, Kwangsi Province, the place where my mother first began her missionary career.

TOWED UP

THE WEST RIVER

We arrived in Liu Chow around 6 p.m., tired and hungry. Mother was excited, as this was the city where she had spent her first two years as a missionary with the Christian and Missionary Alliance (C&MA), studying the Mandarin language. I remember Mother standing in the marketplace deciding which direction to take to the C&MA headquarters. Mother finally got her bearings and led us to the C&MA compound.

Mr. Desterhoft answered when we rang the bell at the big gate. He exclaimed, "Praise the Lord! You received my letter and you have arrived!" Again we saw the Lord's hand directing us, as we had certainly not received Mr Desterhoft's letter. In fact, we had received no mail for more than two years.

Mr. Desterhoft had written an urgent letter to my parents, requesting them to teach the senior class in the South China Bible College in Wuchow. Mr. Newburn, the college president, had returned to the United States on emergency furlough. Even though my folks no longer served under C&MA, the South China Field Council decided that my parents, with their command of the Cantonese language, were the only missionaries in that part of South China qualified to fill the emergency void. The Morgans continued north, finally arriving in the United States in April 1943.

We Barnetts had a few days of much-needed rest in real beds at the C&MA headquarters before heading up the West River by towboat to Wuchow. A tugboat towed a couple of barges up the river beside the mountains. When the current became too strong, human power for towing was necessary. Two groups of 18 men, one set on each side of the river, climbed in their bare feet over the rocks of the rugged mountain which came down to the river's edge. It was scary watching them pull our barge, but they were extremely sure-footed. The last lap of the journey was completed in a large motor launch, which the missionaries nicknamed the "Blue Bottle."

The South China Bible College was located on a mountain island in the middle of the West River. The "Blue Bottle" reached Wuchow around midnight. I can remember lying on a grass mat, dangling my hand in the dirty river water, and watching the oil lamps in the small, flat-bottomed boats, called sampans, as they flickered like little fairy lights against the darkness of the jungle-covered mountain. My father had to barter with the sampan owner to take us across to the Wuchow mountain village.

Although something like 15 years had elapsed since Mother last visited, she was able to locate the path up the mountain to the mission headquarters and the Bible College. It took us almost an hour to reach the top of the mountain. The big iron gates were locked, but Mr. Henry Holton was watching to meet and welcome us. He let me peek at little four-year-old Genevieve, asleep under her mosquito net. We were then ushered to a beautiful guest room—with real beds—on the second floor. I could hardly wait until morning; I had much to explore.

Life on the mountaintop was exciting. My parents' days were taken up with preparing and teaching in the Bible school. Genevieve and I played house and enjoyed campus life. For the first time in years, I ate three meals a day in a formal dining room with linen tablecloths and napkins, an incredible luxury.

The peaceful college setting was often interrupted by the sound of temple gongs echoing from mountain to mountain, alerting the communities that enemy planes were on the way.

The second warning was sirens, letting us know the planes definitely were headed our way. The third warning was whistles, to let us know bombs would be dropping on us. This could happen any time of the day or night.

At the second warning, everyone headed for the caves partway down the mountain. To us children, this was exciting. There were plenty of places in the jungle tunnels and caves to play "hide-and-seek." My parents thought the trek was a waste of time, as it always seemed to follow a false alarm.

One day everyone fled except my parents. I decided to go and join the fun. My white hat and red sunsuit made me conspicuous to the airplanes. I ran to the top of the little cliff overlooking the mission graveyard. The air-raid shelters lay beyond this point, and the cliff was too steep for me to go around. I lay down and covered my ears as the screaming silver bombs streaked through the air. The planes were so low, I could see the pilots's faces. The bombs exploded, but not close to me.

The Japanese actually were aiming for a military installation on the next mountaintop, and it was easy to mistake the Bible school buildings for their target. In between the waves of planes, I heard Uncle Henry Holton calling my name. When I peeked over the little cliff, he said, "Jump!" I jumped, and he caught me. We made it to the shelter before the next plane came over. This time they hit the boys' dorm. Somehow after this event, my parents changed their minds. And when the alarm sounded during the day, they headed for the caves. At night, however, they decided their sleep was more important.

I have wonderful memories of Wuchow, surely one of the most beautiful places on Earth. The trips down the mountain island to the West River took about half an hour. There we bartered for a sampan to transport us across the swift river to Wuchow City, where we could spend our money.

My parents received a monthly stipend for teaching, enough to buy a bar of soap. Since that purchase was not needed every month, there was extra to spend on the most precious gift I could imagine: a beautiful marble. Among all the merchants with their wares spread out on the side of the road was an elderly man selling all colors and sizes of glass marbles. It took me ages to make up my mind which one to buy. My parents showed great patience with my deliberations. A pretty marble still brings me great enjoyment today. I have a glass jar in my classroom where I store special marbles my students bring me.

Another benefit of living in Wuchow was fellowshiping with other missionaries. The outstanding memory I have of devotions each morning was the singing of hymns. The Hill family often joined us, and I remember Mrs. Hill's beautiful voice singing "He Lives," her favorite song.

A frequent guest at the Bible school was the famous Dr. Wallace. He made sure that Genevieve and I got our daily requirement of calcium by grinding into powder toothbrush handles which, at that time—at least in China—were made of bone. This doctor devoted his whole life to caring for the Chinese people before he was martyred for Christ in the 1950s.

s e v e n

OVER THE HIMALAYAS

As time for graduation at the South China Bible College approached, the bombing grew both in intensity and frequency. The faculty decided to give final exams on the tombstones of the missionaries in order to keep the students closer to the air-raid shelter. The graduation ceremony itself took place after the war.

Now it was time for us Barnetts to continue our journey across China, hoping to reach India and a ship to the United States. This journey would take us over four more months. Mother and I left Wuchow by train for Kueilin with Mr. and Mrs. Hill, their two-year-old son, Elston, and their three-week-old baby boy. Included in our party of eight was Mrs. Bert, a blind missionary to the blind. My father had gone to another mission station to see about acquiring travel money.

The train offered only sitting or standing room, not both. We took turns sitting on the board benches. Mrs. Hill and Elston both suffered high fevers. The only food on hand was soup we purchased through the window whenever the train stopped near a village. This situation continued for days.

We chugged along through the jungles with people packed inside, on top of the train, and even lying on the fenders over the wheels. Many overloaded trains had traveled this one and only route to freedom. The weak who could no longer hang on, dropped off by the tracks. Their corpses and skeletons assailed our eyes—and noses—as we made our way to Kueilin.

In the meantime, my father was successful in his venture, but was unable to board a train to catch up to my mother and me.

The Lord has means of providing, even in comical ways. Somehow my father found a G.I. uniform that fit him. It was no small matter for an ex-Royal Air Force airman to don a Yankee outfit, but he did. With this, he was given a private compartment on the next train.

Where were Mother and I by this time? Sitting in a smelly, dirty, broken-down train a couple of days away from Kueilin with no hope of rescue. Our train engine broke down right by a double track, which meant that the next train could travel through safely. When it spotted our train, the oncoming one slowed down. A mass exodus ensued as passengers from our train scrambled to board the passing train for a chance to survive.

The slow-moving train was gone before Mother and I could move. I stuck my head out the window to watch the passing train when I spotted my father sitting in comfort in his private compartment. It was too late for us, but long enough for him to see where we were. When he reached Kueilin, he bargained with the engineer to go back with his engine and pull us safely to freedom. We didn't know at that time that our days of freedom were numbered. Ten days later, Kueilin was destroyed by fire.

My parents and I finally reached Kueilin. Walking down the wide main street of the city, we saw bombs exploding in the distance. We found the partially bombed-out compound of the Braga family, whom we knew. What a welcome sight! When we cleared out the rubble, Father and Mr. Hill found locked trunks in the attic.

Since we had nothing, we broke the locks to find bedding, including mosquito nets; cooking utensils; and dishes. There were plenty of bricks around to build a *funglo* (Chinese stove), and plenty of wood for fuel. A nearby street market provided the basics for a hot meal. That night, as sick as she was, Mrs. Hill could still sing "He Lives."

My eagerness to explore never waned. Outside the Bragas' house, I found what must have been beautiful formal gardens, complete with fountain and walks, although now overgrown. As I made my way along, I stumbled across a little bird, hopping around because it could not fly. On closer examination I could see a big hole in its throat. For several days I visited it with water, most of which came out through the hole. My final visit was for a burial. War brings human suffering, but we often do not think of the tragedy that results, because of selfishness, to all of God's creation.

The day of reckoning fast approached. The Americans—Mrs. Bert and the Hill family—were given passage to India on an American plane. They had to promise to repay the cost when they reached India. My father, being English, was refused passage; Mother and I chose to stay with him. We just committed everything to the Lord. He had brought us this far with miracle after miracle performed on our behalf.

At 3 a.m. on the eighth day of the evacuation period the Japanese had designated, a knock at the door announced the presence of a jeep, provided by the British Embassy. They would fly my parents and me out to Kunming. Did we ever scramble around in the light of the peanut oil lamp!

Before we left the Bragas, Father purchased new locks for the trunks and replaced all the borrowed items with a note of thanks. The Braga family had passed through our part of South China as refugees and we had cared for them, so we knew they wouldn't mind returning the favor by sharing their things with us. In fact, years later in Hong Kong, we shared many enjoyable times with them at their cottage at Castle Peak. Stuart Braga and I climbed the ceramic dragon in the formal gardens of the estate his father built.

The day of our flight was wet and drizzly, but nothing could dampen my parents' and my high spirits. We boarded an 18-passenger Royal Air Force plane with bucket seats on either side of the aisle and little round portholes to look out. After a short time, the pilot decided the fog was too thick to take off since mountain peaks rose sharply on all sides. We would have to wait until tomorrow.

My parents and I spent the night in Army barracks, great fun for me. I weighed only 35 pounds at the age of eight, and plenty of military daddies who were lonesome for their children back home were only too happy to carry me over the muddy areas to meals. They even took turns watching over me during the night. This is where I learned the most amount of English in the shortest span of time. The men gave me a candy tin with sugar cubes in it, a treasured gift.

The following morning, my parents and I again boarded the airplane. The weather was still too dangerous for flying, but our pilot gave us two choices: try it and possibly crash on a mountain, or stay and be burned up. We had less than an hour to decide. One look at our competent pilot's face, covered with scars from war wounds, and we all decided to go. He said, "Fine, but you must leave everything on the runway to lighten the load."

I wondered if we might leave behind the 200-pound lady. Everything of ours, except Father's 16mm camera with film, Mother's five-year diary, and my precious tin candy box with a picture of a girl and her horse on the lid got left on the runway. I managed to spirit off a couple of very special marbles in my pocket, too.

After a prayer, we strapped into our seats and it seemed as though we went straight up. What a surprise! In no time at all, we were bathed in welcome sunshine. The weather was so perfect that we only had to fly at 18,000 feet instead of the usual 26,000. The cabin was not pressurized; the air was thin, with no extra oxygen to spare. Several people passed out, but no one dared move from their seats. By late afternoon our pilot, with the Lord's help, landed us safely in Kunming in a rainstorm.

My parents and I were met and cared for by wonderful friends of the China Inland Mission (CIM). Baths, clean clothes, warm meals, and beds were such luxuries! The Lord not only spared our lives, but also gave us all this unexpected comfort besides. In the meantime, the Japanese dumped gasoline on Kueilin, the city we had left behind, and set it ablaze. More than 100,000 people perished.

Our sleep was interrupted at 3 a.m. again, this time by a message from the British Embassy saying my parents and I were allowed to fly to India in the same plane, leaving in just two hours. Our clothes were ironed dry while we ate breakfast and prayed. Away we went in the jeep to board our plane. The scenery was breathtakingly beautiful as we left Kunming. We flew right alongside the Himalaya Mountains, so close it seemed as if we could reach out and touch them.

We stopped to refuel in Rangoon, Burma. The airport sat in a desert-like place, without a tree or house in sight. After our fuel was brought to us, our little plane had to taxi in line, waiting our turn to take off in between the bombers, which left at the rate of one every three minutes.

Meanwhile, the heat was almost unbearable. We all stood in the shade of the plane's wings and waited our turn to refuel, a two-hour period. Mother had been given a couple of large, juicy pears when we left Kunming; and when we took them out of the plane, we found they were almost frozen from the high altitude flight. We divided the pears among all 18 passengers, grateful for the thirst quenching they provided.

Finally, it was our plane's turn to take off. It was rather scary as our plane was so small and the roaring bombers so large. But again, the Lord was with us. We soared up like an eagle on the last lap of our flight into India.

e i g h t

INDIA:

LAND OF CONTRASTS

Arriving in Calcutta, India, we Barnetts were tired and hungry, but grateful to the British for our free ride to safety. We now faced several hours of customs inspection. The American government personnel were now anxious to talk. They wanted to debrief my father because of all the miles we had covered since leaving our home in South China.

An American military doctor first gave us physicals. Years later we met Dr. Dean Smith when he took care of my grandfather in Grand Rapids, Michigan, and learned that he was in Calcutta, India, in August 1944 when we arrived. He looked after the refugees coming over the Himalayas from China. He remembered the name Barnett, and how skinny the three of us were.

Although we were penniless, the U.S. military was so eager for information that they offered to pay our way across India to Bombay. What more could we ask? We were loaded on a train in our own private compartment—upholstered entirely in leather—for the ride to Delhi, India's capital city. When the train stopped at mealtimes, our meals were handed in on silver trays. In between meals, my parents and I were offered tea and cookies.

Everything was great until nighttime. As soon as the lights went out, we had visitors—huge cockroaches. Mother sat up all night with a flashlight, trying to keep them off me. Their saw-like jaws left painful bites. In spite of these extremes, we made it to Delhi, where we were met and put up in a hotel for 10 days.

After supper in the hotel dining room, we were entertained on our balcony by a huge group of monkeys of all sizes. It was interesting to watch the little babies clinging to their mothers' backs. They seemed friendly, coming right up to us, looking for food.

A good night's sleep was a real treat. Father and Mother got up by 5:30 a.m., as usual, to read their Bibles and pray. Because it was warm, they left the balcony door open. Father was in the bathroom shaving when a gorilla about four feet tall walked in. Mother watched in her usual calm manner as the gorilla tried to waken me. Then he spotted Mother's purse. He emptied the contents on the dresser but could not find any money.

Next the animal found my prized tin candy box. He could probably smell the sugar cubes. Attempting to open the can by throwing it on the floor proved unsuccessful. Meanwhile Mother prayed silently, not daring to make a sound. The beast decided there was nothing to gain staying around, and left to find better worlds to conquer. Mother quickly shut the door behind him and thanked the Lord for keeping us from harm.

Father came in, I woke up, and Mother had quite a tale to share. Hidden behind the drapes we found a little sign which read: "Beware of monkeys trained as pickpockets." It seemed that each hotel had its own trained crew of simian thieves.

Around 10 a.m., a limousine arrived to take my father to the American Embassy, where he recounted our experience with the gorilla. We were promptly transferred to a British boarding school, where we were catapulted into high society. We had existed on a near starvation diet for over two years. Now we were fed seven times a day. The program went something like this:

6:00 a.m. Silver tray laden with tea and biscuits (cookies)
8:00 a.m. Breakfast in the formal dining room
10:00 a.m. Tea and rolls served wherever we were
1:00 p.m. Lunch

4:00 p.m. High tea (sandwiches)
7:00 p.m. Formal dinner where the head Indian waiter
dressed in white, a gold sword at his side
10:00 p.m. Tea and fruit

Every time we turned around it seemed like it was time to eat!

My father rode in limousine each day to U.S. military headquarters for top-secret debriefings. One of the results of his talks was that planes were secretly sent to rescue French women and children still in the French Indochina area. All 80 of them were brought out safely. This was planned with the French vice-governor, who had helped my family and the Morgans to escape.

My father, with the Lord's help, made the correct guess as to where to bomb the Japanese. We heard later that every time the Japanese moved their headquarters, they got bombed out! Father also told the Americans that if our compound were bombed by mistake, he would send them a bill later. One pilot sent back word that he left his "calling card"—a spray of machine-gun fire on our back wall. Sure enough, when we returned in 1946, we found the row of bullet holes and had a good laugh.

During our 10 days as guests of the U.S. military, my parents and I were taken to see some of the historical sights of Delhi, such as the Lal Kila (Red Fort), off-limits for civilians at that time. The palace and grounds were exquisite! I remember walking through the main part, where each square foot of the marble floor had precious stones inlaid.

Having completed our assigned task in Delhi, we were sent to the Central Province to a girls' school of the Ramabai Mukti Mission, where Miss Bernice Steed, a missionary from our home church in Grand Rapids, Michigan, worked. We were sent to the orphanage to recuperate and to await transportation to the United States.

We needed the rest, as my father weighed less than 100 pounds, my mother in the 80s, and I weighed less than 40 pounds. We were fed water buffalo milk and had clothes made for us. Aunt Bernice gave me a little china doll that was about three inches long. I kept it in a little oval basket complete with a tiny little blanket. What a treasure!

It was fun going places with Aunt Bernice. One afternoon we walked quite a long distance to an Indian Christian's home for dinner. Aunt Bernice and I were dressed in saris, a colorful piece of cloth six yards long, wrapped around and pleated in front to make a long dress, the loose end of the material thrown over one shoulder. It was fine while walking, but when we arrived at the home of our host, that was a different story. We were invited to sit cross-legged on the dirt floor, made of packed buffalo dung and mud, and the large, layered pleats in the front of my sari refused to bend.

To make matters worse, I was hungry and the aroma from the curry smelled delicious, but when I gulped a mouthful, it burned all the way down. Indians eat very hot, spicy foods. I'll take Chinese food any day!

We stayed more than a month, being refreshed in body and spirit. After leaving Mukti, my parents and I traveled to a private home in Bombay to await booking on the next ship going to the United States. The spacious mansion, nestled in a tropical jungle setting, stood a short distance from a beach with pearly white sand that extended as far as the eye could see. We swam in the Indian Ocean twice a day. Sometimes during the night, we heard a tiger roaring. It was comforting to know that guards kept watch over us.

A strange custom took place in that palatial home. Our bathroom floor was ceramic tile with a step leading down into it. Each morning around 10 a.m., servants stripped the beds, gathered all our laundry, flooded the bathroom floor, and scrubbed the clothes there. When the wash was done, they bailed the water out and mopped up the floor. The clothes and bedding were laid out on the grass to dry. All would be returned, neatly ironed, by noon.

The American Embassy sent instructions for us to board a ship for home. The name of our ship and exact destination would remain a secret until we reached the United States.

FORTY-SEVEN DAYS
OF BLACKOUT
BEFORE FREEDOM

After weeks of waiting and uncertainty, the day finally arrived for us to board a huge troop transport along with hundreds of others bound for the United States of America. When would we sail? When would we arrive at our destination? What was the name of the ship? Only the Lord knew the answers to those questions, and what the next 47 days would hold for all of us.

The place of our departure was the ancient city of Bombay, India; the time was the end of August 1944. All of us on the ship had survived the war and anticipated arriving in a free country, but a few did not live to see that day.

On the eve of our departure, people rescued from a ship that sailed a few days before us reached Bombay. The enemy sank their ship, and they spent days on a raft in the Indian Ocean. Would we go through the same experience? Psalm 37:5 says, *"Commit thy way unto the Lord . . . ,"* and that is what we did.

The ship was like a little city with its own hospital, stores, church, theater, and recreational areas. The women and children were quartered on "B" deck, with the men below. Each cabin held 18 people in three-decker bunks. Of course, we older kids scrambled for the top bunk. It was fun sleeping up there until the sea became turbulent. Then some of us appeared with fresh bruises in the morning.

This ship had strict rules for us to follow. From late afternoon until mid-morning, all doors and portholes were sealed tight, and all dim lights in the cabins and corridors were draped with black cloth. Throwing anything overboard was strictly forbidden, and the ship traveled a zigzag path. All this was to help prevent the enemy from locating us. Two destroyers escorted us through the Indian Ocean.

While the grownups did all the worrying, every day was filled with excitement for us kids. We were allowed to play only on parts of certain decks on certain days. The troops had a good time teaching us how to chew a strange thing they called gum, and there was always plenty of candy in their pockets. My favorite G.I. carried me to "civilian-restrictive areas" and explained parts of the huge ship to me. This entertainment lasted until he was reprimanded for his kindness.

Twenty-four hours a day we all wore big, heavy life jackets. Every few hours the siren to abandon ship rang and, no matter what time of day, we all had to report to our assigned lifeboat stations. We never knew whether it was the real thing or just a drill. All families were split up; I was assigned to a lifeboat full of troops.

One day a torpedo hit our ship. When I arrived at my assigned lifeboat station, the abandon-ship siren still sounding, the lifeboat had already been lowered. Someone picked me up and threw me overboard; a man in the boat caught me. By the time the lifeboat reached the water, some sailors down in "D" deck had risked their lives and closed off the safety doors, thereby saving the ship.

Since there were so many people on-board ship, the two meals served each day were eaten in assigned shifts. Each shift had 15 minutes to finish a meal before the tables were cleared for the next sitting. If anyone missed his assigned time, he went without his meal.

There was great excitement when we learned we would see

Australia. As we passed through the Great Australian Bight, one of the roughest ocean spots of the world, it really "bit." Many of us were seasick. We dropped anchor at Melbourne. It was wonderful to be near civilization again, even though we were not allowed ashore.

Up the coast of Australia is the city of Sydney, where we made an unscheduled stop. It was a sad day for all as we watched a missionary couple go ashore to bury their only child, who had died the night before.

The 400 civilians on-board, about half of them missionaries, spoke many different languages. Playing "hide-and-seek" in different languages posed quite a challenge! We children soon adopted parts of all the different languages, resulting in a speech of our own. Communication was clear to us, although it often kept the adults guessing.

A bulletin each day updated us about world situations. Heated discussion often broke out among the women in the cabin as to what happened on a given day, since days blended together because of the blackout. Mrs. Bert, the blind missionary who had traveled with my parents and me in West China, stayed in my cabin. She could settle any argument, blackout notwithstanding, because she pecked out each bulletin in braille as my mother read it to her. The blackout did not hinder her!

Scheduling use of the big hall for meetings was a complicated process. Separate services were held for Catholics, Jews, and Protestants. When no religious services were being held, movies were shown or checkers tournaments held. I beat a Catholic priest in one of the checkers tournaments. I remember the time a woman was asked on a Friday night to sing at a Sunday service. She planned to practice on Saturday, but when she woke up, the next morning was Sunday! We had crossed the International Date Line and lost a day.

We often wondered how far along we were on our journey. As long as the sun rose at the front of the ship, we knew we were headed east. But one day it rose at the rear, and we knew something was wrong. We learned we were bound for New Hebrides to pick up all troops, dead or alive.

When we docked at Espiritu Santo, thousands of soldiers marched aboard all night long. Hundreds of coffins were also loaded. The wounded were transported to the ship by ambulance, and lifeboats carried them up to the hospital on "A" deck. I will never forget the afternoons when some of us girls visited these men. One had lost both arms and legs. He told us about his little girl, whom he had not seen for three years.

One afternoon the long-awaited message blared over the loud speaker, "Tomorrow we will see our beloved United States of America!" After the announcement, the "Star Spangled Banner" was played. One elderly missionary lady fainted at the top of a flight of stairs and fell head-first, landing at my feet. She didn't live to see the "Land of the Free" but, instead, went to meet her Savior and enjoy her eternal home.

Forty-seven days after my parents and I left India, our ship, the U.S.S. *General Butner,* as we now learned our ship was called, glided into harbor at San Diego, California. Ours was the first ship in nine to reach the United States; the others were sunk by Japanese torpedoes. Bands welcomed us.

We watched for hours as the troops marched off the ship. We were told there were over 5,000 of them, many suffering from shell shock. The wounded were lowered in lifeboats, and ambulances waited to carry them away. Then came the solemn procession of steel coffins draped with American flags, containing the remains of those being brought home to their loved ones for burial. At last the civilians were allowed off, and as we stepped onto dry land, we thanked the Lord for a safe trip to a free country.

It was early afternoon when my parents and I disembarked from the *General Butner.* The American Red Cross provided food and cots that sustained us through the long customs period. All the civilians were placed in alphabetical order in roped-off areas. Baggage was not a problem, because most folks wore everything they owned. Aunt Bernice Steed had given us a suitcase when we stayed with her in India. She had also made me a blue-flowered dress out of one of her dresses, and I was saving it for the day we arrived in Grand Rapids, Michigan.

Since our last name started with "B," my parents and I only had to wait an hour for our name to be called. As Father opened the suitcase, you can imagine our surprise to find all ladies' things. Fortunately, a lady with a last name starting with "B" called out, "Where's my suitcase? I have someone else's." Lo and behold, the identical suitcases somehow had gotten mixed up back in the ship's cabin.

Even though our suitcase was almost empty, it took five hours for the customs official to go through the contents. We had 16mm film taken on our 10-month, thousands-of-miles-long journey. The thing that held us up longest was my mother's five-year diary. There were parts in which she had written with a piece of coal when no pen or pencil was available. The customs officer finally admitted he could not find any forbidden information, but that it was so interesting he could not put it down. He finally gave it back and handed us over to the Red Cross. We were free!

The Red Cross contacted our home church, Wealthy Street Baptist in Grand Rapids, Michigan. You can imagine their surprise at this news, as they had been told we were missing. They wired money to us, and the Red Cross put us on a train headed east.

The trip to Michigan took five days, which we spent sitting on bench-like seats. We often were bumped off for troops and had to wait in train depots for the next train. We were used to going days without a bed and having little to eat, so even this was better than the past. We were headed home!

Arriving in Chicago on a Wednesday evening, Father had

enough money to pay for soft seats in a special train car. This gave us a chance to wash up, and I changed into my special "Aunt Bernice" dress.

We must have been about half an hour away from Grand Rapids when I asked my mother, in Chinese, of course, "When will we get to America?" She tried to explain but was overwhelmed by the realization that we were almost at our journey's end. It just did not seem possible.

Around midnight our train pulled into the Grand Rapids Union Station. Would there be anyone to meet us? The next thing I remember is blinding flashes of light and being passed from one person to the next. Father and Mother were lost in the crowd. The platform and station were packed with people wanting to greet us and members of the press eager to take pictures and ask questions.

It was the wee hours of the morning when we arrived at my great Uncle Martin and Aunt Naida Cummiford's farm on 60th Street and Kalamazoo Avenue. Yes, we had arrived in the United States of America.

AMERICA:

WHAT AN EXPERIENCE!

I will never forget my first night sleeping in a bed in America. First of all, I was used to sleeping on bed boards, but that night I had to share a soft bed with my mother's cousin, Gladys. I didn't dare move because I thought I would bounce out. After Cousin Gladys went to work early the next morning, I slid carefully out of bed and enjoyed a wonderful sleep on the floor underneath the bed.

By the time I woke up, it was almost 11 a.m. I had no idea where I was. I looked out the window and could not believe my eyes. In America even the trees were painted! No one had ever told me about autumn colors, and that wasn't something I'd ever seen in China.

Venturing out of my room, I found stairs, and went down. I met my Great Aunt Naida and asked her for my *aba* (father) and *ama* (mother). She spoke rapidly, but I could not understand English to begin with, so I did not know what she was saying. I found out later that Miss Brumler from church had taken my parents to buy us some warm clothes.

Aunt Naida gave me something to eat. I remember thinking, *What strange food.* It wasn't rice, and in the Far East, if you haven't had rice, you haven't eaten a meal. Oh well, my parents and I had eaten plenty of strange foods in the last three years, and I wasn't about to complain.

At one meal, Aunt Naida served strawberry shortcake. I refused to taste a single bite. Mother was so upset with me, she sent
me to bed. No one understood that I thought the whipped
cream was soapsuds. I had begun to get accustomed to all of the
strange habits of Americans, but I thought eating soapsuds was
just too much!

Those first few weeks on the farm were glorious. My cousin,
Ellen, was 15 and the two of us did many things together. She
taught me how to play croquet and do many farm chores; we
gathered eggs in the barn and fed the animals. We even slept in
the hayloft. Then came the time for the trees to shed their leaves,
and I got to play in the piles of leaves. In the tropics, leaves
remain green. Here there were "naked" trees.

At my family's official welcome home at Wealthy Street
Baptist Church, more than 1,000 people attended. I thought the
receiving line would never end. Aunt Jeanette Brumler came to
my rescue and took me upstairs to her office. There on her desk
sat a huge box containing the most beautiful doll I had ever seen,
dressed all in pink. It was love at first sight. I named my doll Judy,
after a new friend, Judy Zoerhof. For the next few years, Judy
(the doll) went everywhere with me, either carried in my arms
or strapped to my back like Di Goo, my *amah,* carried me when
I was a baby.

Not too long after this, I saw my first snowfall. It was as if
cotton fell from the sky and covered everything. Cousin Ellen
pulled me on a sled, which I thoroughly enjoyed, but putting on
all those clothes and boots was a pain. I was used to sunsuits and
bare feet or *kecks* (wooden flip-flops).

My ninth birthday and the Christmas of 1944 were spent in
North Quincy, near Boston, getting acquainted with my grandparents, Mr. and Mrs. Clay Church. They lived in a little bunga-
low one block from the Atlantic Ocean. Mother and I often took
long walks up and down the beach. A mile up the beach was an

Air Force station where we liked to watch the huge dirigibles dock.

My favorite Christmas present that year came from my Uncle Bob, my mother's brother. He took me to pick out a kitten, my first pet in the United States. Her favorite trick was to get a running start from the kitchen, tear through the living room, and land in the middle of the Christmas tree. She made a fuzzy little ornament, hanging there meowing for help.

In early 1945 my parents and I returned to Grand Rapids. My parents were on furlough, speaking in many different cities. During this time I stayed in the home of Pastor and Mrs. David Otis Fuller. Their daughter, Beverly, was like the big sister I never had. Then there were two boys, Alan and David, to contend with. Baby Mabel was just like a little doll. Mrs. Fuller always walked me down the street toward Oakdale Christian School. She showed her kindness in other ways, such as giving me a chest rub when I had a cold.

At that time, Dr. Fuller was a chaplain in the U.S. Navy, and away from home. When the phone rang on Sunday afternoons, we all lined up to talk to him. Dr. Fuller also was a member of the board of the Association of Baptists for World Evangelism (ABWE). He suggested that my parents serve under a mission board such as ABWE rather than remain independent missionaries. My parents agreed, and traveled to Philadelphia, where ABWE was headquartered.

When my parents arrived in Philadelphia, who should meet their train and welcome them to ABWE but Jay and Dorothy Morgan. The Morgans had beaten the Barnetts in the transition from working as independent missionaries by joining ABWE that very morning. When my parents were accepted by ABWE, the two couples were assigned as co-workers in the same city.

After my parents returned from Philadelphia as official ABWE missionaries, we moved into a home on Bates Street, completely furnished by our church. As we walked in the front door, I heard the back door close. We walked into the kitchen and there on the table, set for three, stood a dish of hot Spanish rice. Our first meal in our new American home was delicious! I always wondered who made that special delivery.

I chose a room upstairs with a big double bed, where I was less likely to fall out. Father put a board under the mattress so it would not be so bouncy. The house had three bedrooms, a bathroom, and a linen closet filled with beautiful fluffy towels and bars of fragrant soap.

Downstairs was the large living room, a dining room, my father's office, and a kitchen with dinette. A little room by the back door, where the milkman delivered milk, also held an ice box in which the iceman deposited a huge hunk of ice every other day.

The basement contained a wringer washing machine and lines on which to hang clothes indoors, an oddity to me. I was accustomed to seeing laundry hanging out-of-doors. I found a good use for the indoor clotheslines, however. On second-hand roller skates, I learned how to skate, holding onto the clotheslines.

The scariest part about living in America, to me, was attending school. At nine years of age, I could not read English, so I was placed in second grade in Oakdale Christian School. I walked the several blocks with my friend Ruth Harrison, who attended the nearby public school.

I was way ahead in math, but could not read a word or understand what was being said. I was sent up to a little room next to the principal's office "to learn to read." I sat there, waiting for the prescribed half-hour to go by. I recall a man in the next room, sitting with his feet propped on a huge desk. He waved once in a while, but that was about all. At least he was a friendly principal.

Years later I met that same principal, by then the admissions director of Calvin College. He was shocked to hear of my long-ago experience in his school. It reminds me of the story of the teacher who sent a new non-reading student to a reading teacher. After a few tests, the reading teacher sent the student back with a note which said, "Sorry, I can't do anything with your new student. He can't read!"

Recess was another trying time for me. The other students all touched me to see if I felt the same as they. I guess they figured if I could not speak their language, I must feel different, too. One day I had enough and ran home. My mother gave me a spanking and sent me back to school. The saddest part was that recess had just finished, so nobody even missed me.

I do have some good memories of my short stay at Oakdale. I learned my first two hymns in English, and gradually began to understand spoken English. My teacher read the story *Heidi,* the highlight of my school day. I could sort of make up the story from looking at the pictures.

During the summer of 1945, Mother took my friend Ruth and me on the streetcar to John Ball Park Zoo or out to Reed's Lake Amusement Park. A ride on the paddle-wheeled steamboat with player piano was exciting. We paid one price for as many times around the lake as we wished. We often ate a picnic lunch on these outings.

In August my parents and I attended Niagara Bible Conference, where my father was the keynote speaker. A side trip to Niagara Falls almost ended in disaster. We innocently walked with the crowd past the halfway point on the International Bridge when a guard asked to see our identification. My parents and I had left our passports at home. When we said that Father was born in England and I was born in Hong Kong, we were taken into custody. Finally, the pastor of a church where my father was to speak came and bailed us out in time for the evening speaking engagement.

Back at Niagara Bible Conference grounds, I had my first encounter with baseball. It was August 14, 1945, and I was up to bat when someone ran down the road screaming, "The war is over!" At that announcement, so was the game.

That fall I entered third grade in the public school in North Quincy, Massachusetts, where my parents and I had moved for a while. Although our class was a handful for the beautiful, young, first-year teacher, she was very kind to me. After I left, she sent me a beautiful sterling silver locket with little pink flowers. I do not remember her name, but I do remember and appreciate her kindness. Maybe she is a little part of the reason why I became a teacher.

During this time in Massachusetts, on Thursday afternoons after school, I attended a Bible club in Elizabeth Chisholm's basement, a few doors from my grandparents' home. It was she who explained the way of salvation to me, going over the Bible verse in John 1:12: *"But as many as receive Him, to them gave He power to become the sons of God, even to them that believe on His name."* That afternoon I accepted Christ as my own personal Savior.

From that time on, I knew that I belonged to Christ. It did not matter what lay ahead; I could trust Him to guide my life. Little did I know that I would face death many times, but always with the confidence that I would go to be with the Lord. Neither good works nor anything else is needed to get a person to heaven. That was an exciting day in my life.

Later that year, Dr. Paul Jackson baptized my cousin Ellen and me at Wealthy Street Baptist Church.

e l e v e n

HEADING HOME

With the war over, Father wasted no time in applying for passports and visas in order for the three of us to return to China. On January 1, 1946, we were packed and ready to leave Boston for Grand Rapids. As we said goodbye to my grandparents, a special delivery letter arrived containing the necessary passports and visas. God's timing was just right once again!

We arrived in Grand Rapids for a farewell shower at the church. And what a shower it was! More than 20 trunks and suitcases were required to hold all the gifts the church gave us. It took much planning to prepare for four years of living 12,000 miles away. Figuring out how much toothpaste, vitamins, and medical supplies we'd need both for the clinic and for us was quite a challenge. John and Louise Cederlund, who owned a local pharmacy, gave us much of what we needed. It was a big chore calculating just how much of everything—clothes, school supplies, and equipment—would be necessary, and an even bigger chore to pack it all.

Finally, my parents and I were ready to leave from the same train station we'd arrived at two years earlier, with numerous friends to bid us Godspeed. I loved the train ride across the United States, quite different from the ride during the war. This time, we had comfortable seats, beds to sleep in at night, and ate our meals in the dining car.

There was always plenty to do, and the five days passed quickly. At one station where our train stopped, we got off to stretch our legs. Another train stood on the adjacent track. My parents got back on the train without me. When both trains began to move, I could not tell which one was ours; I just jumped onto the slower train. I walked through car after car, looking for my folks. I found them reading a book, not in the least bit worried. They thought I was in the next car. I learned my lesson: never lose sight of your parents.

We arrived in Seattle, Washington, to news of a dock strike; our ship would sail from San Francisco instead. Mother and I stopped in Oregon on the way to San Francisco to see her Aunt Ferne, who owned a chicken hatchery. How strange to see little baby chicks hatching in incubators instead of under a hen!

In San Francisco we met with a pleasant surprise. ABWE missionaries Robert and Grace Kohler, with two girls near my age, were headed for the Philippine Islands. A nurse whom we called Aunt Jean was also part of our ABWE mission family. All of us would travel together on the same ship.

Before sailing, Father was able to purchase a short-wave Halifax radio that not only brought enjoyment to many on the ship, but also proved invaluable during the unsettled years yet to come.

Our trip of about three weeks across the Pacific was calm and uneventful until we reached Manila on February 4, 1946. Ours was the first ship to arrive in the capital after World War II. The harbor was still full of sunken ships. There was one dock, but no one to unload the ship of about 600 passengers.

Mr. Edward Bomm, ABWE's business manager in Manila, met us in his jeep. He and his wife, Marian, had survived a Japanese concentration camp during the war. Most roads were not cleared, and most buildings had been bombed out. The city government was still collecting unexploded bombs and had bodies to bury. Tents and army barracks served as living quarters. We ABWE missionaries-in-transit were housed in army barracks with American troops.

The day after our arrival in Manila, when Mr. Bomm, Mr.

Kohler, and my father went to see about our baggage, they found the ship unloaded. Everything had been dumped on the dock in one big heap—hundreds of pieces of luggage, a good share of them broken open. It took several days to locate all our belongings, but all 23 pieces of luggage were found intact. Again, the Lord protected.

Life in the barracks was far from dull. The Kohler girls and I found plenty to entertain us. One evening after supper, we had a race back "home" to our barracks. Lou Ann stumbled inside the door and knocked over the fire extinguisher. White foam poured out and, in no time, we were perched up on top bunks watching the floor become covered foot-deep in foam. A guard heard our screams and came to our rescue. Rest assured, we three were punished for that escapade.

One of the best adventures I remember in Manila occurred with the nurse, Aunt Jean. She found a bombed-out hospital with usable equipment lying everywhere. She, the Kohler girls, and I spent hours collecting and cleaning things Aunt Jean could use in her clinic there in the Philippines.

Each morning, all the missionaries met in Mr. and Mrs. Bomm's tent, which became ABWE missionary headquarters. I remember the theme song we sang together after prayer each morning: "Sweet hour of prayer, sweet hour of prayer, that calls me from a world of care. . . ." Outside, as far as the eye could see, was nothing but destruction, but inside the tent was a resting place "from a world of care."

My father finally located an inter-island steamer named *The Mactan,* headed for repairs in Hong Kong. It carried about 100 passengers, and my parents and I were fortunate enough to get a "cabin." It held a board-shelf bunk bed, and had enough space in which to unfold a camp cot after the door was closed. We left Manila on March 5, 1946, expecting to arrive in Hong Kong three days later. Instead, it took 11 hair-raising days.

Our first day out in the South China Sea was a beautiful

cruise past tropical islands. As we neared the top of Luzon, the captain reported that we were running out of drinking water. We dropped anchor in a peaceful bay. My father and others went ashore, where they found fresh water on the edge of the jungle. That emergency taken care of, we again sailed out into the South China Sea.

Then, without warning, the sea began to churn. Passengers who were on the deck had to be strapped down in the dining area. My parents and I hibernated in our cabin where we strapped ourselves down. We had no food or water, and did not dare open the door. After a couple of days, we heard a knock on our single porthole.

When the ship rolled to the opposite side, Father opened the porthole to reveal a Chinese fellow, clinging to the side of the boat. A Christian man and a member of the crew, he had risked his life to bring us food: water, cold rice, and dried shrimp. Once in a while, he brought a candy bar. Although I was grateful for the provisions, to this day I do not care for shrimp.

The days wore on. The sky was clear, but the ocean was unbelievable. No one knew what was happening. Father twice read me the story *Paula, The Waldensian,* by Eva Lecomte, to pass the time. Mother became very ill. Finally, 11 days later, we dropped anchor in a beautiful bay with pearly white beaches. Where in the world were we? We were all thankful to have survived; not a single life had been lost.

By this time the boat listed heavily to one side, although it was still sailable. Father went up on the bridge to talk with the captain. The unbelievable story he reported back to Mother and me was that the captain did not have a map of the South China coast, and was guessing his way to Hong Kong! He forgot that Hong Kong was without electricity, and how does one find a city nestled among tropical mountain islands?

Around 8 a.m., a fishing junk pulled up near our boat. Father called to the fishermen, one of whom came aboard *The Mactan.*

He spoke Cantonese, so Father translated for the captain, who was a Filipino. They bargained for the junk's services to direct our boat to Hong Kong.

We learned we had landed in the most notorious pirates' den on the South China coast. *The Mactan* had not been attacked because the pirates thought we were a decoy for the British, who had been cracking down on piracy since the end of the war. The pirate's price was high. He wore the same size as my father, so he wanted a white suit, shirt, belt, shoes, socks, and money. He also demanded a guarantee of freedom when we reached Hong Kong. There went Father's only white Sunday suit and shoes.

It took us another half day of sailing to reach Hong Kong. This harbor, too, was full of sunken ships, and the colony had suffered extensive bombing. The lack of electricity explained why we sailed right by the city the night before.

Our pirate pilot hired himself a water taxi and disappeared before we sailed into Hong Kong Harbor. Without docks, we anchored in the harbor itself. The water was still rough and it was quite a chore to load our large trunks into sampans. It took many trips for us to get my family and our baggage safely on land. Then we had to locate a hotel. Rickshaws were the means of transportation, and it took 10 to get my parents and me—and all our luggage—to a Chinese hotel. Then Father had to rent one room just to store all of our baggage.

We were so thankful to be alive! We finally learned what had caused the incredibly rough seas. The "birth" of an island in the Pacific Ocean, 1,000 miles away, caused tidal waves that disrupted the seas. More than 1,000 people drowned in Japan, and there was terrible destruction for thousands of miles around the Pacific Rim. We were fortunate to have been spared. God directed our paths once again.

The following morning (Sunday), Mother was not feeling well, so Father and I set off without her to find a church. We came to the place on Caine Road where the church should have been, but all that remained of the building was a heap of rubble. We were walking along, trying to identify landmarks, when an excited voice greeted us. It was the C. S. Wong family, who had taken care of our house in Chek Hom. We thought they were still in that city. Again, the Lord knew our needs before we did.

When the Wongs heard that we were staying in a hotel, they kept me with them and sent their private rickshaws to bring Mother and Father to their spacious apartment, up on Hong Kong Mountain. They had a servant go to the hotel to watch our trunks until they could be moved on Monday. That evening, Mother became even more ill, and the Wongs called a doctor and nurse to take care of her throughout the night. The doctor said Mother probably would not have lived until morning had we stayed in the hotel. The Lord still had work for Mother to do.

We stayed with the Wongs for several months in their beautiful home with its lovely gardens. Mr. Wong worked for an oil company and certainly provided us with the best. It was in stark contrast to the destruction in most other areas of Hong Kong.

My parents and I were only 250 miles away from home, but could find no boat to take us there. Finally, the way opened up for us to go overland through Wuchow, where we lived during World War II. This meant riding on the towboat up the West River. Of all things, Dr. and Mrs. Oldfield (the man who ate my peanuts), now in their seventies, were also returning to Wu Chow. The five of us traveled together on the barge.

The mountains on either side of the river were rugged and steep. In some places the current was so strong that the little tugboat needed help. We eventually transferred to what the missionaries nicknamed the "Blue Bottle," a ferryboat that took us the rest of the way to Wuchow. We spent the night in a Chinese inn within view of Wuchow Mountain. I wanted to go up, but it would have meant several hours of climbing and we had to catch a "bus" at 5 a.m.

Early the next morning found us in a Chinese village wait-ing for our bus. We did not leave until 11 a.m. because we had to wait for an important passenger who had been attending a wed-ding. I had my doll, Judy, strapped to my back. She drew a large crowd that my folks were able to tell about the real God. They pointed out that my doll, Judy, was like their idols—with a mouth that could not talk, eyes that could not see, and ears that could not hear their prayers.

It was a dry, hot day and the clay dirt left red dust on every-thing. The bus was open at the back where the passengers sat on board benches, packed in like sardines, along with baskets of chickens and their personal belongings. The few suitcases my parents and I brought along with us were tied onto the roof. The man who was late getting on the bus sat me on his knee in the cab. My poor folks tried to breathe through handkerchiefs; they were covered with thick, red dust. What a sight!

Because of our late start, we had to spend the night in a vil-lage along the way. After finding an inn, getting washed up, and eating a hot meal, Father and I took a short walk. It was Wednesday evening, and you can imagine how surprised we were to hear the strains of the old hymn "What a Friend We Have in Jesus" in that remote little village in South China. A group of Christians were meeting for prayer in a home.

It is hard to put into words my feelings the next morning, knowing that was the day I would arrive home! Somewhere Father managed to find a car going to Chek Hom. That ride was a luxury compared to the rickety, dirty old bus.

HOME AT LAST

Around 3 p.m. on April 24, 1946, my parents and I arrived at the bottom of Kai Ling (Chicken Hill). First out of the car, I tore up the hill to the small gate at the bottom of our compound. I pulled the chain that rang the old bell. I could hear the slats on the doors being pushed. When they were opened, there stood a pleasingly plump Chinese lady I did not know. What should I do?

She took one look at me, and at the top of her voice proclaimed, "Hallelujah!" She threw open her arms, and I ran in, even though I did not know her. The Wongs' oil company put this lady in charge of our property, and she raised pigs for a living. Oh my! Everything looked so different. The servants' quarters had been made into pigpens. A bamboo fence now divided the lower part of our compound from the upper part where the house stood, probably to keep the pigs in.

I tried to find one of the walks that led up to our house at the top of the hill. Everything was overgrown and our beautiful lawn had been dug up to be replaced by sweet potato plants. I stood there, finding it hard to believe this mess had once been our beautiful home. Oh well, when Father and I got to work on it, it would soon look much different. At least we were home!

I waited for my folks to catch up before I entered the house. The Wongs lived there after we left, and then the Japanese used it. Now it was vacant and dirty, with broken windows and missing screens. Cleaning and setting up housekeeping did not take long. We had our folding cots and mosquito nets with us, and I found an old orange crate for a stool. It felt good to be back in my own room again.

Word of our arrival traveled fast. Within an hour, friends arrived, each one bringing a gift of food or returning something of ours they had hidden from the Japanese. It was amusing to see dignified Mr. Lai, in his flowing mandarin robe, walking up the garden path with our wastebasket in his hands.

The Lo family brought us supper. It was great to see my playmates, Chee Kwun and Wing Lok, again. The Los stayed for part of the year before returning to their home in Canton. During this time we children made up our own language so even our folks did not know what we were saying.

These were busy days with sweet potatoes to dig up and a lawn to lay. Underground tile pipes to the septic tank had to be replaced before the bathtub and sink were usable again. The Japanese had stolen our toilet, so another would have to be purchased in Hong Kong and shipped to us. The screens for all the windows had to be custom made. The list of things to be done seemed endless. I wouldn't start school until our trunks were shipped from Hong Kong anyway, so there wasn't anything else for me to do.

The biggest job we faced was planting the vegetable garden. We raised most of our own food because it was not safe to eat anything raw from the Chinese market. In China, human waste was used as fertilizer, and that practice transmitted numerous diseases on unclean produce.

The Chinese church in Chek Hom was still going strong. During the war, they had met in homes. Now they would meet in our house until they could rebuild the church building. Our living room was large, and the big French doors opened out onto the verandah. The overflow was accommodated out in the garden. Those sitting on the verandah had to avoid the pigeons, as four sets of rafters had been claimed by the birds after the Japanese occupation.

I remember one Wednesday evening when the church service was interrupted because a sow at the bottom of our garden was giving birth to 23 little piglets. What could be more important, when we had just prayed for her safe delivery.

The rest of our belongings finally arrived from Hong Kong, and my schooling resumed. Although I was past 10 years of age, Mother ordered a second grade Calvert correspondence course from Baltimore, Maryland. The easier work was necessary because of my sporadic schooling and the catching up in English comprehension I still needed.

Father and I got up early each day and watered the garden by hand. Then Mother and I completed my lessons before the stifling heat of the day set in. Typical temperatures reached over 100°, with humidity in the high 90s. Under those conditions, doing much of anything—let alone concentrating or studying—was next to impossible. That made an early start imperative. No sleeping in at our house!

These first years back at home were both peaceful and exciting. I resumed friendships with my Chinese friends in Chek Hom, my parents picked up their work with the two local congregations, and our property was restored to its former orderliness. If not for those killed in the fighting and the emotional toll taken on those who survived, it was almost possible to forget that the war had ever taken place—almost.

t h i **r t** e e n

UNRRA

COMES TO TOWN

We were back to business as usual on Kai Ling (Chicken Hill). The sweet potato garden had been converted back to a lawn. Father was even able to locate and buy back our old push lawn mower. We now could set up and play croquet and other games which we enjoyed.

One day a rumor in town reported a "foreign devil" had arrived in the seaport of Fort Bayard, 10 miles away. When one of our friends passed on the news to us, Father rode the old charcoal-burning bus out to Fort Bayard to see what information he could gather.

In the meantime, we were having an exciting day back in Chek Hom. The bell rang at the lower compound gate, and there stood the "foreign devil" Father had gone to find. He had heard about us and came to get acquainted.

The man was Mr. Frier, an old acquaintance of my father's from back in England. Mr. Frier now worked for the United Nations and was stationed in Fort Bayard to oversee the distribution of tons of food and goods. It was a monumental task, requiring someone who knew the area and the need, and who spoke the language. In my parents, Mr. Frier found the help he needed to get his huge task off the ground.

A few days before Mr. Frier's arrival, my father and I had been downtown in Chek Hom buying bread when we noticed unmarked, brown cans in a store window. No one knew where they came from or what was in them. We turned a can over and read "USA," so we bought one. When we opened it for afternoon tea, you can imagine our surprise to find the can contained pork and beans. They were delicious, even though we knew it had to have been stolen. No doubt they came from the *godown* (warehouse) where the United Nations Relief & Rehabilitation Association (UNRRA) supplies were stored.

Mr. Frier stayed at our house until Father returned late in the afternoon. The two men had quite a reunion! Since Father had been unable to find the mysterious "foreign devil" in Fort Bayard, he paid a visit to the Chen family and found they had the Morgans' old dog, Penny. Patches, the Morgans' other dog, had run away the morning after their servant left town, so the Chens rescued Penny. We had a double reunion that afternoon. Penny, old and thin, lay in exhaustion on our verandah, at times trying to muster enough strength to wag her tail in gratitude.

After this, my parents and I looked forward to Mr. Frier's visits. He brought practical gifts for Mother, such as a set of teacups. Our only remaining cup with a handle was given to the guest of honor. Living inland like we did, household items were hard to replace.

It was exciting for me to accompany my father to Fort Bayard to spend the day with Mr. Frier. He and my father worked on plans for the big relief distribution project. Mr. Frier lived on the compound of what had been the old governor's mansion. He had acres of land in back where he was testing seeds from the UNRRA shipment. He had servants to tend the gardens and servants inside the mansion. We always had such delicious goodies for high tea, another name for British supper.

When Mr. Frier found out that my favorite was canned pears, he kept a can for me in the larder, or pantry. Sometimes I napped on his bed—a big, high four-poster that needed steps in order to reach it.

Mr. Frier had been given use of the governor's mansion

because the district had a new Chinese governor. Now that the French had given the territory back to China, the Chinese governor decided he needed a new mansion. A graduate of the University of Michigan, the Chinese man returned to the area to govern and get rich. He told my father that he moved to a different district every two years or so. That way he could bleed the new area and get rich quicker.

When my father's and Mr Frier's plans were put into action, it generated great excitement. Father, two helpers (Titus and Mr. Lai, a Bible school student), and I rode the bus from Chek Hom to Fort Bayard. After a visit with Mr. Frier, we all traveled in his jeep a few blocks to the warehouse. The UNRRA provided three shiny new trucks that were loaded with barrels of bean powder, hundreds of cases of dried milk powder, pork and beans, bales of cloth, many pounds of buttons, and hundreds of 200-pound sacks of rice.

Titus, Mr. Lai, and I each had a truck to guard to keep people from stealing as they were being loaded. Father stood at the door of the warehouse to direct the loading process.

One time, as a coolie emerged from the warehouse with a heavy sack of rice on his back, a member of the gathering crowd plunged his knife into the burlap sack. The rice flowed onto the street. The people lunged forward, and we had a riot on our hands. Father, his big black umbrella in hand, went after the crowd, reprimanding them in Chinese. He drew a line on the ground. He told the people that if they stayed behind that line, they would be given all the rice they could carry home. He also asked for volunteers to help with the distribution.

Everything went smoothly, and we received the much-needed help. It was worthwhile to see the happy faces of people filling their hats, shirts, and anything else they could think of in order to carry home the unexpected treasure. More than 100 people went away with several days' wages worth of rice.

The 10-mile return trip to Chek Hom over the bumpy dirt

road was no fun. Each of us still had a truck to patrol as we stopped in little villages along the way. Sometimes when standing at one end of the truck, we had to scramble over the stuff to stop someone from stealing a five-pound can of powdered milk out of a case at the other end. There was never a dull moment.

Finally, at the end of a long day, we arrived at the top of Kai Ling. The "road" ended, and the trucks had to drive carefully across the top of our hill on boards laid over the washout points. They maneuvered through our big gates close to the garage, where the cargo was stored.

Distribution was another story! Thousands of refugees in their grass and mud huts shared our hill and any other available spot. Many of these people were well educated. They had been uprooted from their homes in northern China and lost everything during World War II. Mother and Mrs. Wong went from hut to hut taking a census, delegating one member to collect for each family, and getting his or her thumbprint to match up on the specified day of distribution.

I will never forget the first mass distribution, lasting three days from sunrise to sunset. The recipients lined up all the way down the hill, entering in one gate and exiting out another. They had to produce their tickets, to match against the information in the record book, and give their thumbprints again.

Preparation for the three days was no easy task. Everything had to be measured. Bolts upon bolts of cloth had to be ripped, folded, and piled according to the number of people in the family. This left some of us with very sore arm muscles.

My favorite job was counting out buttons on the tiles of our living room floor. My least favorite job was being scrubbed from head to foot, puting on my bathing suit which Mother had sterilized by boiling, and being placed in a barrel of dry bean soup powder to dig out the last two feet that had hardened because of the humidity.

I survived, even though it took hours with so many barrels

to empty. I was not allowed out until the specified amount for the day was chopped loose, as Mother would have to scrub me all over again. When my father came to check on me, he also brought some news. I learned of Mahatma Gandhi's death in India, on January 30, 1948, as I stood in a barrel of soup powder.

Another event connected with the dispensing of the UNRRA relief supplies was shocking. I strolled down the hill to greet the people in line when I came across a young mother with a two-year-old. I played with her little daughter. Then the mother said, "I must go home, but I will be back."

A few hours later, I saw her in line again, this time with her newborn son strapped to her back. Yes, she had gone home, delivered her own baby, and returned to receive her relief goods. When I told Mrs. Wong, she personally gathered the young woman's relief goods and took her home. That young mother later became a Christian, and we were able to locate her husband and help reunite them in Singapore.

Although thousands of families received aid, it hardly made a dent in the huge shipments the UNRRA sent. Father found a way to get the rice out to the needy. He found highly educated men in the village to organize groups of 100 men. They went through the villages repairing washed-out roads. In this way, the whole area was cleaned up, and each worker received a day's wages in rice (about one pound) for a half-day's work.

While Mr. Wong used our property during the war, he installed an 80-foot-deep well. After one of the little piglets fell in, Father decided the well needed to be filled in. It wasn't much use anyway, as we were too high up on the hill to get much water from it. While investigating, Father discovered the well was lined with thousands of first-quality fired bricks. He hired a man to remove them. After around 1,500 bricks were removed, we looked down and spotted the digger—a mere speck on a ledge near the bottom.

It was hard for Father to convince the man to come up and

leave the remaining bricks, despite the danger of a cave in. The man protested, but finally relented. Then Father assigned 400 men to go out on the hillside and build a new road leading to the village. They dug a deep trench for rainwater run-off so the road would not wash away during the rainy season. The extra dirt from the trench was used to fill in our well.

The work took several days, but it was a resounding success. When the job was finally completed, the men were grateful for the rice they received as payment, the community enjoyed the new road, and our well was filled in. Those 2,000 bricks were worth a fortune. Later they were used to build rooms for the Bible school students, plus other important projects, such as my playhouse foundation and floor.

f o u r t e e n

NEW ARRIVALS

On January 15, 1947, my parents received a telegram stating that the Morgan family had arrived in Hong Kong. Days went by before we learned, again by telegram, that they would be coming to Tsam Kong (the new name for our district) on a ship, the *Toi Shan*.

The next news we heard was a radio report that the *Toi Shan* struck a floating mine and sank, with loss of life at 150 or more. We did not know if the Morgans were among the casualties and waited for over a week before we received a telegram which said, "Arriving tomorrow aboard the Maple." At least we now knew the Morgans were alive, but no one knew what the Maple was. My father managed to discover that UNRRA had a tugboat called *The Maple*.

Sure enough, on January 29, 1947, Father and I stood on the pier in Fort Bayard, 10 miles from home, as *The Maple* arrived bearing the happy faces we had waited so long to see. The Morgans had traveled down the South China coast from Hong Kong, over 250 miles of open sea, on an 80-foot tugboat with all their earthly possessions tied down on the fantail.

I remember the first thing Aunt Dorothy said to me was, "Oh, you have hair!" She said when I was little, my hair was very thin, and she had worried about me. Now my hair had grown thick and long. For this special occasion, Mother had tied my hair in rags the night before, so I sported long curls down to my waist.

Immediately after the Morgans' trunks, crates, and bundles were unloaded from the tugboat, we were free to leave for Chek

Hom. The Morgans already had passed through customs at a small station just outside the territorial waters of Hong Kong. This small customs station had been established to accommodate the sea-going junks and other small craft traveling up and down the South China coast. In Chinese it was called Laap Saap Mei (the end of the garbage).

My father hired a truck and some coolies to handle and transport the Morgans' baggage (which included a crated kerosene refrigerator, trunks, and bicycles) to Chek Hom from Fort Bayard. We drove the 10 miles inland to Chek Hom in our 1935 Chevrolet automobile. It was a thrill for the Morgans to drive into Chek Hom after having been away for more than two years. We drove first to our house on Kai Ling, where Mother had a delicious chop suey supper. Even their old dog Penny was glad to see the Morgans back!

After supper, Mother asked me to go to the chicken coop to collect eggs. I took four-year-old Ann with me. I handed her an egg, but forgot to tell her not to squeeze it. Ann gave herself an "egg bath."

That night the Morgans moved into their new home, a three-story building rented from a dentist and located on the town square.

A short time after the Morgans' arrival, local merchants told us that a small village had suffered repeated attacks from a Bengal tiger. Often kept as cuddly pets by storekeepers when the tigers were very young, the animals grew up to be vicious killers.

When the tiger finally was killed, it was brought into the town of Chek Hom by ox cart to be strung up by its feet on the lower limb of the huge banyan tree growing by the temple in the public square just outside the Morgans' courtyard. Then the tiger was skinned and cut up to be sold to the highest bidders. Every bit of the tiger was sold; hide, hair, tail, and all.

The most expensive part of the tiger was the heart. Eating that was supposed to make a person brave. The next most expensive part was the tiger's whiskers. Even the bones were sold, to be ground into powder for medicine, or to be made into prized toothbrush handles. The villagers made more money from the sale of the tiger than they had made from their farms for an entire year.

I remember the banyan tree growing in Chek Hom's public square. It was a huge tree from which branch rootlets dropped to form new trees; and it was a perfect place to play "hide-and-seek."

The arrival of the tiger's carcass in Chek Hom was a thrilling event for Jaymes and Ann, and for me. In fact, Jaymes had never seen a tiger up close. That evening, after the bidding for various parts of the tiger, the carcass was lowered to the ground. The villagers had gone into the temple, whether to thank the idols for their success or to drink a bit of rice wine, I do not know. But whatever the reason, the rapid approach of nightfall gave us three children the perfect chance to see a tiger up close, dead though it was.

As we groped our way in the growing darkness around the back of the temple, I tripped and fell—right into the soft stomach of the tiger.

Jaymes called in a hoarse whisper, "Mardie, where are you?"

I answered, "Never mind, just get me out of here!"

Jaymes did not believe me when I told him what happened, so he ran into his house and returned with a flashlight to see for himself. Sure enough, there lay the Royal Bengal Tiger, sprawled on the ground between the town's well and the wall of the temple, waiting to be cut up and distributed to the successful bidders. And there I was, tangled up in the carcass.

f i f t e e n

FATHER, MAY I HAVE
A PLAYHOUSE?

In 1939 in a fishing village called Op Na Kong, on the other side of the city of Chek Hom near the arm of the sea, my mother and I met Grandma Lai picking up sticks with her young grandson, Ha Tsai, whose name means "little shrimp."

Grandma Lai heard about Jesus for the first time that day from my mother. Her wrinkled old face lit up as she said, "That's the name I have been waiting to hear. I have been praying to the unknown God for many years because the gods in the temples are deaf. I wanted this unknown God to make Himself known to me. And now He has!"

It was now eight years after that first meeting, and Ha Tsai came knocking at our door to tell us, "Grandma is very ill. Please come."

Mother went back with him and found Grandma Lai near death in her little grass hut. Nearly 100 years old by now, Grandma Lai had bound feet. This custom prevailed in China for hundreds of years. Little girl-babies' feet were bound so they would not grow properly. Not only did the Chinese find the "little lotuses" beautiful, they also ensured that no bride would run away from her husband, as even walking on bound feet was excruciatingly painful.

Mother made the one-hour walk to Grandma Lai's house every day for several days, bathing and feeding rice gruel to the dying old woman. One morning, Grandma Lai told Mother, "I have two needs. Number one is for someone to take care of Ha Tsai. Number two is for someone to move me to the ground." Chinese custom dictates that a person should die on the ground. I wonder if Genesis 3:19 influenced this ritual.

In any case, Mother shouted in the Lui Chau dialect in Grandma Lai's almost-deaf ear, "I will care for Ha Tsai." Grandma Lai beamed. Then with Ha Tsai's help, Mother moved Grandma Lai off the grass mat–covered bed board onto the ground. Grandma Lai said, "Thanks," and died.

The church people came and buried her. That is how Ha Tsai came to live with my family on our compound. The rice room was turned into his bedroom. I gained a regular playmate, and the two of us always had some big project in the works.

One day I told my father I wanted a real playhouse. I had one—behind the bougainvillea bush that stretched the length of our compound wall—with rooms, and grass mats, and all kinds of things. The bougainvillea bush was so thick it kept out a rain shower. The best thing about this was we could see out, but no one could see in!

But now I wanted a playhouse with windows and a door. Father gave me a corner of the garden where banana, pomelo, lychee, and custard apple trees grew. This corner included the well that was filled in to within six feet of the top. Father said if Ha Tsai and I made our own bricks and built the playhouse against our six-foot compound wall, he would hire a carpenter to build the beams for the tile roof. That was all we needed to hear.

First, Ha Tsai and I made a mold for our bricks. Then we went out on the hillside to dig the red clay and chop long, wiry grass to use in making the bricks. We carried our materials back in baskets on a *domming* (carrying pole). Ha Tsai and I made a two-foot mound of clay. In the center we poured water, laid in the stringy grass, and then mixed the lot with our bare feet. Oh, the wonderful feeling of warm mud oozing between our toes!

We made our own wooden mold, complete with hinges, and molded over 200 bricks. It took days for them to dry, turning them over several times in the hot sun to bake completely.

One night during the drying process, Ha Tsai knocked on my window. "Come quickly!" he called urgently. "A big storm is coming and our precious bricks are uncovered." So there we were at 2 a.m., moving and stacking 200 bricks under the banana trees where they would stay dry.

Once Ha Tsai and I had made enough bricks, it was time to dig the playhouse foundation. We marked it out with string, just like the professionals. Our foundation was around two feet deep, and Father let us use some of the fired bricks he rescued from the well for this part.

Ha Tsai and I made frames for the two windows and the door out of wood salvaged from UNRRA shipments. Finally, the walls went up brick by brick, with the two of us "builders" using plumb lines to keep them straight. Father was as good as his word, hiring a carpenter to put up the roof beams. The tile roof finished off our little playhouse.

The inside measured roughly eight feet by six feet, with the ceiling just over five-feet high on the compound wall side, slanting down to about four-feet high on the opposite side. Ha Tsai and I soon learned where we could stand up and where we could not.

Our final big job was in finishing it off. The walls had to be plastered and whitewashed with a white lime solution that made it look nice and also protected it from termites. We made a door, shutters, and screens. The floor was inlaid with some of the fired bricks from the well, which made an attractive pattern.

With the playhouse completed, it was time for Ha Tsai and me to turn our energies to landscaping. A little bank sloped down from the house to the area of the filled-in well. This we transformed into a rock garden that circled halfway around the well. The other half of the circle had a two-foot wall in front of part of the fence that divided our garden. Pots of nasturtiums showed their cheerful faces, and the low wall made a pleasant place to sit and admire our hard work.

Father cemented the filled-in well to a depth of six feet. Ha Tsai and I then built a four-foot castle of white coral in the well, and added over 200 beautiful tropical fish of every description that we caught in flooded rice fields near the nearby canyons. White water lilies floated on top of the fish pond.

Around the mouth of the old well, a six-inch-high and one-foot-wide ledge held four pots of plants that helped shade our fish from the tropical sun. This well became a place of great beauty, even though it never produced water as was originally hoped.

With our playhouse finished, the landscaping completed, a tropical flower garden planted, and fruit grove cleaned out, Ha Tsai and I proudly surveyed the results of our weeks of hard labor. Many people, especially Mrs. Wong, enjoyed this corner of the compound. She often commented, "It is so peaceful here."

The playhouse itself became useful to others also. It was large enough to hold a cot, so it served as an inn more than once. I guess the most exciting event was the day Ha Tsai was baptized in the garden baptistry made from one of the cisterns that had no cover. From that time on, our little playhouse became a changing room. Ha Tsai—who was given the new name of Ti Daw, or Titus—was the first to use it for that purpose.

Thieves were attracted to the playhouse, as they were to all the buildings on the compound. But Titus and I were prepared for them. Titus strung up cans through the banana trees that lined the walkway to the front door. When anyone tried to pick the playhouse door's lock, the cans all rattled. Our five guard dogs were there almost before the intruders could scale the six-foot wall, where they got plenty of cuts on the jagged glass imbedded in the cement on top before escaping.

The little playhouse and garden gave Titus and me many

first four members of the Kai Ling church (shown in front)

home of explorer ristopher Columbus, noa, Italy

Above:
Wordsworth's house in the Cumberlands, England

Left:
Part of the exotic parade in Colombo

Wong, a new convert "worker"

Marjory's 14th birthday party, her last celebration with the "circle of nine," on December 4, 1949

Marjory on the *Georgic*, 1950

Mr. and Mrs. Bragg, Stuart Bragg, Marjory and Margaret Barnett in Hong Kong

Mrs. Wong, the Bible woman in Chek Hom; Oi Fong, Pastor Chen's daughter; and baby Wing Sang escaped to Hong Kong to establish ABWE's work in 1951.

Marjory on Cheung Chow Island, Hong Kong, in 1950

Our "home," army
barracks in
Manila, 1946

Left:
Chek Hom congregation in front of their new
post-war building

Below:
Marjory in the Chek Hom garden where she and
Titus built their playhouse

ALL ONE IN
CHRIST JESUS

eswick Convention Center, 1950

Marjory and Penny on a camel
near the Great Pyramids of
Egypt, 1950

Marjory, with foster parents John and Louise Cederlund

Marjory in her graduation uniform, 195

Hong Kong missionaries at Marjory's wedding, December 17, 1966. Pictured, from left: Margaret Barnett, Dortha Warner, Starling Post, Ruth Warner, Marjory and Jack Miller, Sharon and Bill Commons, Victor Barnet

Celebrating the Barnetts' 50th wedding anniversary, back row: Margaret Barnett, Marjory, Victor Barnett, Jack Miller; front row: Kathy and David Miller

hours of enjoyment. We had a *funglo* (Chinese charcoal stove) on which we cooked our afternoon rice and *sung* (meat and vegetables to go with the rice). It also was a good, cool place in which to study. The large banana tree leaves that gracefully draped around the entrance offered a shield from sun and rain.

After about a year, we ran into a problem. It didn't take us long to solve it, although it required more hard work. Titus and I had both grown taller; we could stand up only in a small area without bumping our heads on the rafters. We were tired of getting bruises, so we dug up the brick floor. Bucket by bucket we removed dirt, digging down to the depth of one foot. Then we replaced our mosaic brick floor. What a relief, even though we now had to walk down two steps to enter our playhouse.

This whole project was a wonderful learning experience for Titus and me. I derived great satisfaction from making things rather than just receiving them without putting forth any effort to acquire them. That is just one of the many advantages of growing up in a country where toys are not so plentiful.

s i x e e n

MOON FESTIVAL
AND OTHER HOLIDAYS

Beautiful red poinsettias; purple bougainvillea; gold, orange, and wine-colored celosias; white, yellow, and bronze chrysanthemums all announced that fall had arrived in Chek Hom. This handiwork of God was accompanied by the pagan worship and practices of the season, all proclaiming that autumn had arrived in South China.

After the scorching heat and monsoon deluges of summer, fall was a welcome relief. People came from near and far to admire the compound garden we created on Kai Ling.

The Moon Festival was a fun holiday also known as the Double Tenth because it was held on the 10th day of the 10th month (15th day of the 8th month, according to the lunar calendar). Although a pagan holiday when idols are paraded to appease the gods so that they will bless the new crops, the holiday also included making mooncakes and roasting peanuts.

During the afternoons, Titus and I built a clay kiln about three-feet tall from chopped lumps of clay. This kiln, in the shape of a pyramid, sat in a shallow indentation in the ground. It was hollowed in the middle, with air holes around the sides and a large opening on top. Through an opening at the side we burnt the dry sticks and grass we had collected in the morning.

When the clay was red hot, we filled the cavity from the top with large sweet potatoes. With hoes we pushed in the sides and covered the mound with fresh dirt. There the potatoes roasted for several hours. Whoever wanted a roasted potato had to dig it out of the hot dirt. It was worth all the hard work, as those sweet potatoes were delicious!

In the evening, as the full moon rose, people gathered on their flat rooftops to feast and to remember their friends around the world. They were also thankful for a bountiful harvest.

Christians gathered on our front lawn. Under the full moon we held a hymn sing, prayed, and ate a delicious spread of mooncakes, pomelo (similar to grapefruit), roasted nuts, and sweet potatoes.

We Americans observed Thanksgiving, eating a varied dinner according to what was available. According to my mother's diary, in 1946 the main course was pigeon, captured from the rafters of our verandah. Not only did the pigeons provide our food, by eating them we were able to reclaim more seating space for church services. Aunt Dorothy fixed chicken in 1947.

In 1949, my mother had an unusual Thanksgiving celebration in Fort Bayard, where she had gone to visit her friend Faith Snuggs. The communists were shelling all around the city. Mother had just walked out of her guest room to take shelter in the cellar with Aunt Faith when a shell exploded. All they could find upon returning to that room was the leg of a chair; everything else lay in splinters. That Thanksgiving, we were most grateful that Mother and Aunt Faith lived through the day.

Christmas was always a special time for us on Kai Ling. Our flower garden—especially the poinsettias, growing six to eight feet tall—was in full bloom. The children's Christmas programs were delightful. It was a far more spiritual than a materialistic celebration. Christ's birth was the center of the season.

My family celebrated Christmas much as most Christians do in the United States. Father got permission from the governor to cut down a pine tree near the canyons. We made decorations for the tree from hollowed-out eggs. We ate scrambled eggs for weeks before the holidays, as Mother blew out the eggs from a hole in each end to save the whole shells to make ornaments.

We had saved Christmas cards in those days which contained beautiful gold and silver foil paper. This, along with little pictures, made lovely scenes on the eggs. Mother had also saved the metal strips from sardine cans, which were fashioned into icicles. Chains of different-colored papers also draped the tree.

Our presents, too, were mostly homemade, except for a few from the United States which always included a large package of new clothes from the "Airothea Aunties," my mother's Sunday school class at Wealthy Street Baptist Church in Grand Rapids.

Christmas of 1947 was extra special. A large box arrived from the "Fidelis Aunties," another Sunday school class in Grand Rapids. I could read and understand the customs' declaration except for one word: watch. I could not figure out what anyone would be "looking" at in a box. Anyway, I was not supposed to peek, so I did not dare to ask.

Imagine my surprise on Christmas morning! When Jaymes Morgan came up to my house to show off his new present, he announced from the doorway, "Bet I got something you didn't get!" At that moment, we both thrust out our arms—and almost collided. Needless to say, we were both surprised and thrilled with our new watches.

My parents spoke in their old Chinese dialect when they wanted to keep their plans secret. The Lui Chau dialect had been my first language, but it had since faded from my memory. However, Titus spoke this dialect, so he helped me re-learn the necessary amount to keep me out of the dark. It paid off when I caught whiff of a pending trip to Fort Bayard. I worked hard to complete as much of my schoolwork as possible. My parents couldn't use that as an excuse to leave me behind.

Sure enough, one morning after my dad and I watered the garden by hand, Father announced, "I need to make a trip to Fort Bayard."

I asked, "May I go along?"

The answer I had anticipated came from my mother. "No. You have school work to do."

I knew better than to contradict her. Instead, I asked, "If I have a couple of days' work done, would I be able to go?"

She said, "Sure," not realizing I had been getting up at 4 a.m. and tiptoeing out to my playhouse, toiling by the light of a peanut oil lamp to get ahead. When Mother checked my work and found I had completed almost a week's studies in advance, Father and I went to Fort Bayard on the old charcoal-burning bus.

Father's reason for traveling to Fort Bayard was the notice he had received to appear at customs. The item turned out to be one of Aunt Jeanette Brumler's famous packages. The declaration slip read "Used clothes." Aunt Jeanette wrapped her packages in layers and layers of mosquito net, each layer sewed by hand.

Father told the customs officer, "You are welcome to inspect the package, but please do not destroy the netting."

The official started to pick at a few threads, but eventually gave up. Father was able to claim the package without paying much in import fees.

Since it was a very hot day, I asked the customs officer for a drink. He took me back to his house where, while waiting, I recognized *National Geographic* magazines on the table. Before we left the customs house, I told my father what I'd found.

He innocently wondered aloud, "Has anyone seen any *National Geographic* magazines? I'm missing 11 back issues."

Of course, no one had seen any of the missing magazines. But soon after that trip, our missing magazines began arriving in Chek Hom.

Once Father and I returned home, we could hardly wait to open Aunt Jeanette's package. Only the top layers were sewn; it didn't take long to carefully unwind the much-needed mosquito netting.

When Father dumped out the used clothes, out rolled a tin

of cookies. Then two boxes, the first one labeled "Angel Food Cake." I had never heard of such a thing. If that was not enough, the next box said "Devil's Food Cake." I laughed so hard, my side hurt. My mother's attempts to explain the whole thing to me in Chinese did nothing to stem the flow of my laughter.

Chinese New Year is a major holiday in China, a sort of national birthday celebration when everyone is a year older. It's the biggest holiday of the year for Chinese people. Children are given money in a red envelope and a pinch on the cheek. By the end of the day after visiting friends with my parents, both of my cheeks were bruised! But it was worth it. I didn't get much sleep with firecrackers booming all day and night, but New Year's only came once a year.

Easter was my favorite time of year. The night before, Mother tied my hair in rags and on Easter, my long curls cascaded to my waist. The day began with a sunrise service on our front lawn as the sun rose over the bay of the South China Sea. Our hilltop garden was in full bloom. The familiar hymns of "Christ the Lord is Risen Today" and "Christ Arose" know no language barriers; they are loved the world over.

There was a time of prayer and thankfulness for a risen Savior, and deep contentment in knowing that my parents and I were part of the means God used in spreading the gospel message in this part of China.

seven**n**teen

TIME OUT AND
TEMPORARY EVACUATION

The Morgans and my parents worked hard, and the Lord blessed their endeavors. Several churches were established and, by this time, the Bible Institute was in full swing. Mother and Mrs. Wong held a medical clinic in the morning and taught night school for children who worked in the firecracker factories 10–12 hours a day for 10 days in a row before getting a day off. Everyone stayed busy!

Friday afternoons were set aside to hike to the canyons, where we kids ran free and played while our folks held business meetings to plan future work and to discuss and solve any existing problems.

The canyons, a half-hour's walk from home, were made of packed sand in every color of the rainbow. They were like colored fingers that reached into the cliff from a crystal clear, sandy-bottomed river. There were plenty of scary pinnacles to climb (Jaymes always beat everyone to the top) and grassy slopes to roll down. It was so hot that, within a few minutes after splashing in the river, we had completely dried off. Ann loved to fish for minnows with a butterfly net in a fishing hole; or we would all go hunting for *dwonnies* (a tasty berry that grew on low bushes).

Years later when Jaymes and I studied at Hampden DuBose Academy in Florida, my father showed some colored movies of one of our trips to the canyons. Mr. Cole, the geology teacher there, told us he had studied about these rare canyons of southern China but had never seen any pictures of them. I was blessed to grow up in a place of unusual natural phenomena.

Sometimes the Bible Institute students accompanied us to the canyons. We had great fun watching to see pleasingly plump Mrs. Wong squeeze through the narrow pass that snaked its way down into the canyon from the fields above. She went sideways and held her breath in narrower parts. She was always a good sport!

It was wonderful to be able to enjoy the beauty of God's creation. Often, as we left, the setting sun painted the sky in a blaze of color, reminding us of God's care.

Spring of 1948 brought warning of trouble ahead. On one Sunday, my father went to Lui Chau City in an armored car with General Tiet Dom (whose name means "iron courage"). The general was a friend of my father; he knew Father would be interested in checking on our property in Lui Chau.

Because he had a severe headache, Father decided not to go. Soon after the others started out, an ambush killed the general and his men. The Lord had a purpose in allowing my father's headache—it saved his life!

Sunday, May 23, was a beautiful day. The Herndons, missionary friends, were visiting us on their way to Hong Kong. Their son, Norman, and Jaymes Morgan spent the afternoon throwing a soft oblong object at each other on the hilltop behind our house. I could not figure it out. They did not kick the thing, and it wasn't round. When I threw it, it went in one direction and bounced in another. They called this strange object a "football."

All of us ate dinner together at the Morgans' house, and I stayed to play with Ann while my folks went back home for the open-air service on our hilltop.

Jaymes, Ann, and I helped set up wooden benches in the Morgans' courtyard for their open-air service. Ann and I sat on the front seats next to Mr. Herndon. Uncle Jay preached from a board suspended over two benches. For some reason, I whispered to Ann, "Let's move back a row." We did.

Immediately after Ann and I moved, a stone thrown by a slingshot hit Uncle Jay below his right eye. He fainted and would have fallen right on top of us girls, except Mr. Herndon broke his fall. The stone had been thrown by a communist agitator hiding in the dark of the banyan tree by the temple across the street.

The crowd dismissed and we went inside the Morgans' house. Christians gathered to pray as a doctor was summoned to bring bleeding under control. I remember sneaking out in the courtyard and finding a jagged stone with blood on it. Meanwhile, my father walked down to the Morgans' to find out why I hadn't come home. He was shocked to hear the news, and joined our prayer vigil. The walk all the way through town and up our hill was scary, even with my father's big flashlight. But the Lord saved Uncle Jay's life, and saw my father and me safely home.

Because of intensified persecution, all of us foreigners, after receiving the series of five shots plus a smallpox vaccine required to enter Hong Kong, were evacuated there until things settled down. On June 28, my parents and I left for Hong Kong with the Morgans by way of Canton. Recent floods had washed out the bridge on the Chek Hom–Fort Bayard road. To get across the river, we paid strong men to use wedges and hoist the bridge's cement slabs to water level so the bus could drive across. It was precarious, to say the least.

Traveling up the South China Sea on a motorized junk, the seven of us slept on the flat cover to the cargo hold, giving us an astronomer's dream of viewing the stars without city lights to interfere.

Once we reached Canton, we changed to a sleek steamer bound for Hong Kong. Before we set sail, we had a surprise visit from the Lo family. I talked with my childhood friends, Chee Kwun and her brother Wing Lok, catching up on everything that had happened to them since they left Chek Hom in 1946. My old playmates now had a little brother named Josh.

I always enjoyed visiting the Crown Colony of Hong Kong. I often stayed at the C&MA hostel for missionary kids, to see my friend Mary Notson. We rode the cable car up Victoria's Peak. Fellow passengers clapped when they saw our long braids sticking straight out, as if we conjured the spectacle just for them. In any case, the Peak Tram provided a thrilling ride.

We two girls hiked up to the reservoir on Lion Rock Mountain. Because Hong Kong had no fresh water supply of its own, it relied on water piped in from Communist China and stored water in reservoirs, one of them on Lion Rock Mountain. The piped-in water supply could be curtailed, and sometimes was when the mood struck the communists to do so.

Then the job of obtaining drinking water fell to the children. They stood in line for hours in oppressing heat in order to fill their allotted containers with drinking water for the whole family.

Another exciting trip was the launch ride to Cheung Chau Island, shaped like a dumbbell, with a ball at each end. A Chinese fishing village was located in the narrowest part, with private stone cottages dotted over the larger ends. Since my parents stayed at different cottages in the 1920s and 1930s, they had a lot of stories to tell.

One cottage, called the "Captain's House," was built on a rock by a sea captain. The living room looked like the bridge of a ship, and commanded a magnificent view of the islands and the South China Sea. The Morgans and my family stayed at the Russo House, along with missionary families from other parts of China. All the missionaries present gathered in the evenings on the flat rooftop to sing. One man played a mouth organ, while another played his accordian.

There were so many places to explore on the island. Early mornings found most of us swimming at the Morning Beach, where the tide crashed in on the big rocks. Afternoons were spent on the beautiful sandy Evening Beach. I can remember one time Jaymes was out swimming and ran into a Portuguese man-o'-war, a large jellyfish, that stung him from head to toe. Although injured, Jaymes' life was spared.

My family returned to Chek Hom where I plodded along with Calvert correspondence courses during the day and Chinese school in the evening. It was at this time I memorized four of the *Confucius Classics*. Each one teaches a lesson. The first one I learned tells about Confucius traveling with his followers over the mountains when he hears a woman wailing.

The men asked her, "Why are you wailing?"

The woman replied, "Tigers killed all of my family over the years."

The men then wondered, "Why don't you move to the city?"

To which the woman replied, "There is bad government in the city."

Confucius admonished his disciples, "Oppressive government is worse than tigers!"

Why were these words of wisdom so soon forgotten in China?

eighteen

A BURST OF
MACHINE GUN FIRE

The doctor warned my father in November of 1948 that if he had another attack of malaria, he probably would not survive. The attacks came every year on the same day in February. One day Father would be desperately ill, and the next he would be up hoeing his garden. This pattern continued for several weeks until he regained his health. Because he needed immediate medical treatment and we were low on food, my father decided to travel to Hong Kong.

Father left on December 6th by way of Canton, since there was no direct booking to Hong Kong. His motor junk was late getting into Canton, and he arrived just as the launch for Hong Kong was leaving. He was not allowed to board, so he found passage to Hong Kong on a British gunboat the next day.

Meanwhile on Sunday, December 19th, in Chek Hom, Mother attended the Kai Ling church, and I went with my friend Lum Kiu to the church in Chek Hom. After church Lum Kiu and I walked over to the Morgans' home. We noticed hordes of troops in the center of town, dressed in Nationalist uniforms but carrying red handkerchiefs tucked in their back pockets. They appeared to be moving into the hotel, the tallest building in town.

When Lum Kiu and I reached my house, we found my mother talking with the principal of an elementary school in the living room. We girls settled down to our favorite pastime:

sewing doll clothes in my bedroom.

Suddenly our peaceful, calm afternoon was shattered by what sounded like gunfire. I told Lum Kiu, "It must be fire-crackers."

She laughed and said, "I thought you would be scared."

We went on sewing until a burst of machine gun fire came from the army tower, only 200 feet from our compound gate. That was too close for comfort!

I knocked on the living room door. I opened it to find Mother and her friend on their knees praying.

Mother said, "Can't you see we are praying? Please don't interrupt us."

I said, "But, Mother . . ."

Just then, another burst of gunfire sent all four of us diving for safety under the dining room table.

After we got our bearings, we realized we would be safer under the kitchen table, so we crawled in there. We could hear bullets zooming through the other end of the house. Under the kitchen table we prayed. Mother prayed that the rebels would get scared and leave town. We sang all the hymns we knew—in several languages—and recited Bible verses.

By now it was close to 6 p.m., two hours after the shooting had started. The principal's servant risked her life to find her employer and to notify him that she was needed back at school since looting was expected after the fighting subsided.

Mother, Lum Kiu, and I managed to pull down a quilt to help make the tile floor a little more comfortable. It was here that Lum Kiu told us about her past. Her Buddhist family had all been tailors. She had been sickly in childhood (she was now 16). Her mother went from temple to temple, praying to the idols for Lum Kiu's healing. Each time, the distraught mother was given a coin with a hole in the center. All of them were strung on a red string that Lum Kiu wore around her neck for good luck and healing.

At 15, Lum Kiu wanted to learn how to read, so she attended the evening school on our hill, as she was a seamstress during the day. At our school she heard about the Lord for the first time in her life. Mrs. Wong, our local Bible woman, visited Lum Kiu and led her to accept Christ as her own personal Savior. Much to the consternation of her family, Lum Kiu removed all the coins from around her neck, a several-pound weight. From that moment on, God gave Lum Kiu good health.

Not able to stand up to cook with the continuing rounds of machine gun fire, Mother reached for the last can of pears being saved for my traditional birthday present. The three of us gratefully ate them for our supper.

More than screaming bullets and injured victims serenaded us. Above all this terrifying noise, we heard the students from our two schools scattered across the village that shared our hill, singing their favorite songs. Among them were "Onward Christian Soldiers" and "Jesus Shall Reign." During a lull, the most beautiful sound of all drifted through the fearful darkness as the children sang "Silent Night, Holy Night."

Toward morning, Mrs. Wong crawled on her hands and knees up to our house to see if we were safe. Remember my fishpond? The bottom had dropped a couple of feet when the fill dirt settled; Titus and I rescued our fish and kept them in urns. By using a ladder, the Wongs, Titus, and several Bible school students climbed into the empty fish pond. They spent the night in there on grass mats.

Mrs. Wong brought with her the newspaper that reported the mining of the Canton–Hong Kong ferry. The newspaper said all had been accounted for—dead and alive—except an Englishman in his late 40's. It sounded as if my father might have been killed. We would not know for several more days that he had missed that boat and traveled the Pearl River the next morning, passing the launch and the bodies lying along the riverbank.

My father, meanwhile, was receiving malaria treatment in

Hong Kong. He purchased the *South China Morning Post* and read the headline, "Communists take over Kwangchauwan—all foreigners murdered!" That meant Mother and me, Father thought.

Around noon on Christmas Eve, Mother and I saw Father trudging up the garden path to our house. We acted as if nothing had happened.

But when he reached the door, Father said, "You are supposed to be dead!"

We responded, "So are you!"

We had a good laugh, but also thanked the Lord for sparing our lives once again.

During that night, a few bursts of machine gun fire broke the stillness. Father rushed into my bedroom asking, "What is happening?"

I told him about our procedure. "Just roll out of bed and go on sleeping. Why lose sleep over something as common as a few stray bullets?"

The next morning we had two surprises. Had Mother not rolled out of bed during the night's shooting, she would have been seriously injured or killed, as a bullet had grazed her bed and imbedded itself in the wall. God's protection was evident every hour of the day and night. In a corner of the living room, our decorated Christmas tree stood beneath a place where bullets criss-crossed through the plaster wall. The white dust filtered down, giving the impression of a snow-covered tree. It was the most beautiful Christmas tree I had ever seen.

Meanwhile, down at the Morgans' house, six-year-old Ann had disappeared. She was found hiding between two tall cabinets. When asked why she was there, she stated, "I am hiding from stray bullets!"

ANIMAL FRIENDS

Through the years I had many unusual pets. All the animals lived outdoors because of the sub-tropical climate. When I was four, one of my pets was a turtle large enough to ride. It dug a hole under the wall and left, returning a few months later. This went on for several years until it disappeared forever, perhaps to grace someone's table as turtle soup.

One day while downtown with my father, I was given a calico kitten by the man who owned the local rice shop. I named my new pet Moody. She became my close companion and was allowed in the house during the day.

My parents and I always kept dogs for protection, and Blacky was our first. When we returned after World War II, we found Blacky had run away. I went from village to village, looking for him, but never did find him. He probably ended up on someone's dinner table, as dogs were considered a culinary delicacy in China.

We inherited Dolly, a male dog who had been abused and was, therefore, vicious. He had to be kept tied up at all times. Father would get as close as he could to Dolly, then push the dog's food dish right up to him with a stick. It took six months until the dog would let my father pet him. Later Dolly earned free run of the garden, but he disappeared the moment strangers arrived.

A female Chinese doctor in town begged us to take her black retriever. The dog's name was Sing Lay (victory) because

she was born on V-J Day. This dog had received the best treatment, sleeping in the doctor's house and being fed meat and
other goodies. After we agreed to take the dog, the doctor asked,
"Would you please take one of my cats, too?" I already had
Moody, but we took this extra cat anyway. This woman was the
only doctor in town, but she was leaving because of the threat of
the communist takeover.

Early one Sunday morning my father said, "I have a big surprise for you under the bush in front of the house. Be very careful." When I got on my hands and knees and looked under the
bush, there was Victory with five little fuzzy babies. She seemed
proud of her little family. Victory licked my hand and then her
babies.

One brown puppy, smaller than the others, immediately
became my favorite. I made sure it could reach the "lunch
counter" all right because the bigger pups bunted the runt out of
the way with their heads. When my parents and I agreed to take
Victory, the doctor never told us her dog was pregnant. The next
thing we knew, the cat she gave us had a litter of kittens. We sure
got more than we bargained for!

Around this same time, Moody had three kittens, two calicos
like her and a ginger-colored one. Ann Morgan chose one of the
calico kittens. That left me with a calico named Big Eyes and her
brother, Ginger. He was fat and lazy, and expected his sister to
catch grasshoppers for him to eat, and to wash him.

Big Eyes was a privileged cat because she was allowed in my
room at night. She got in by climbing up to my window, lifting
up the transom with her paw, and squeezing in between the
security bars. Of course, when she came in, she had to bring me
a present. She deposited her gifts under the corner of my mosquito net at the end of my bed. There was no telling what I
would find in the morning.

Often Big Eyes brought me a house lizard; once it was a lit-
tle-bitty chick, not more than a couple of days old. How she ever

brought it through the transom in her mouth without hurting it, I will never know. I woke up to a "Cheep, cheep, cheep."

Inside my mosquito net fireflies twinkled like little stars in the night, while cicadas woke me up with their song in the early morning. A cicada has a life cycle of 17 years. They have three little "jewels" on their head, and a long "tongue" that sucks nectar.

Poisonous creatures, such as scorpions, appeared on our walls. Mother's solution was to take off her shoe, pray, and then try to kill the offensive creature. She had an unbeatable success rate. Fly swatters were useless on scorpions because a scorpion can flex its strong tail and flip off the wall at its attacker.

Once I put on my sock, only to find a huge cockroach trying to chew on my toe. I made sure that never happened again! Centipedes were plentiful, but they were slow moving and usually hid under the dresser. The largest one we ever saw was over a foot long and yellow with age. I actually liked the little house lizards. When I saw one in my room, I could be sure its miniscule white eggs lay close by.

One morning I woke up to see blood on the verandah and sidewalk. I hunted for the source and found Victory sitting on the kitchen steps, holding up her paw to be tended. She had evidently chased a thief over the wall the night before. She must have put her paws up on the solid lower part of the wall, and the thief had reached through the upper part with a knife and slashed the back of her leg clear to the bone. The flesh hung in strips. My mother cleaned the wound, laid the skin over it, and bound it up. Every morning Victory came to the kitchen steps at the same time and waited for her wound to be dressed.

Victory was a friendly dog by day, but after this experience, she did not allow anyone to walk around the compound at night. Thieves beware! We heard Victory chase more than one thief, and I am sure they lost a bit of their legs before clearing the six-foot-high wall that had glass embedded throughout the top. I would not be surprised if some of them later came to my mother's clinic to have their dog bites treated.

In my own fenced-in vegetable garden, I kept a hen and some fertile eggs my father had given me. The hen was set to hatch the eggs, and soon I had 12 little chicks. When they became teenagers, covered with pinfeathers, I needed a chicken coop with a perch. With plenty of wood from the UNRRA crates, I constructed an elaborate chicken coop.

It was arranged so that each morning, with the swish of a couple of buckets of water, the coop was clean. The water drained out into a trough that led to my vegetable garden. The chickens kept the bug population under control, too. Whenever I called to my pet chickens, they perched on my arm. They could not fly any higher because their wings were clipped to keep them inside the pen. When it came time to thin out the chicken population, I went without eating meat that day.

Early each spring, my father purchased a setting duck with ten fertile duck eggs. One time, he even sneaked in a turkey egg he purchased from Hong Kong. When the ducks hatched, they had the run of the compound. It was comical to watch the mother duck with her ducklings following behind in a row— and the "ugly turkey" trying to keep up.

A Chinese colonel came to visit one day. A friend one rank above him owned a pet crane. Since the communist takeover was imminent, the colonel's friend wanted to find a home for his pet, named Deedee. When Deedee stretched out his long legs and even longer neck, he stood around two feet tall.

If Deedee was at the bottom of the compound and I called, "Deedee, Deedee," he came running to get his neck rubbed. He enjoyed our garden, but one day he got too curious for his own good. Over the wall he went and that was the end of his six-month visit. He became soup for someone. We missed his sleek, graceful body gliding in and out of the ferns and flowers.

One morning Big Eyes seemed worried as she led me to a spot under the poinsettias. There lay Ginger, obviously ill.

Mother and I got a dish of water and milk, but he was too weak to move. His dear little sister dipped her paw in the milk and water and put it in his mouth. In this way, Big Eyes kept her brother alive for about one week. We figure someone must have poisoned him. It was a sorrowful funeral Big Eyes and my family held.

The runt of Victory's litter grew up to be one smart dog. I named him Argus, in honor of the dog in Homer's *Odyssey,* which I had been studying. The mythical Argus recognized his master after a 20-year absence, and I hoped that my Argus would prove equally loyal.

One Monday morning during family devotions, Argus began barking loudly at the side of the house. Checking my father's office, I saw a man standing outside the window with a bamboo pole that had a hook on the end. The man was trying to steal my father's Sunday suit off the chair. Argus saved my father's only suit.

Whenever we took out our suitcases to air or to pack for a trip to Hong Kong, Argus laid on the front steps and howled. While we were gone, Mrs. Wong could hardly get him to eat a bite. When we returned, Argus was nothing more than skin-covered bone. I rather doubt that he lived long after we left Chek Hom for good. One lady in the local church did write to say that she took in both Victory and Argus, and shared what food she had with the dogs.

I always wished that I had done what Aunt Faith Snuggs did: put her pets to sleep before she left. It was a hard decision, because my parents and I really did think that, in time, we would return to South China. What we did not realize was that the invasion of Japanese foreigners that enabled us to return to China was quite unlike communism, an invasion from within. In this case, a person's best friend could turn out to be a traitor.

t w e n t y

MUD, STRAW,
AND BAMBOO

March of 1949 was an exciting time; the churches in Chek Hom were growing, and the Bible Institute had its largest enrollment. Life had settled down to relative peacefulness after the previous months of political chaos.

The Morgan family traveled to Hong Kong to meet the new ABWE missionaries, the Jenista family and Miss Loewen, arriving for their first term of service in China. Mother and I prepared our home to receive our new guests, the Jenistas. The Jenista family included Frank and Sophie and their two children, Frankie, two, and Ruthie, one. I remember when Aunt Sophie took out a bottle of Gerber's baby food to feed Ruthie, the little girl looked just like the "Gerber baby" on the label.

After we ate supper and the Jenista babies were put to bed, I had my first baby-sitting job—watching the two little Jenistas—while the adults went to inspect the Jenistas' new home in the city. It was a spacious house with a beautiful garden.

The Jenistas and Miss Loewen stayed with us for a few days until their baggage was uncrated. I loved having them, especially the babies with their beautiful curls. Mother trained Hop Ja, our short-term household helper, to work for the Jenistas. She was such a wonderful person, I was sad to see her leave. But it was good for me to learn, early in life, how to keep house.

First on the Jenistas' agenda—after getting settled—was language study. The new missionaries dug right in, but in six

months, it all came to a screeching halt. The American Counsel
ordered all of us to leave. My father, being English, gave my
family a little leeway; we were able to stay. Everyone else—the
Morgan and Jenista families and the Misses Loewen and
Helsten—left for Hong Kong. The Morgans planned to send
Jaymes to the United States to attend high school at Hampden
DuBose Academy in Florida.

As Miss Loewen boarded the bus to Fort Bayard, a Chinese
lady gave her a present: a brown chicken in a basket. Its head
stuck out through a hole in the basket, and went bob-bob-bob-
bing as Miss Loewen walked along. I always wondered whatever
happened to that chicken; I'm sure it made a fine meal for someone.

The Morgans, Jenistas, and Misses Loewen and Helsten
transferred to Iloilo in the Philippines, where they were badly
needed to teach in ABWE's Doane Baptist Bible Institute.

After all the excitement of packing and saying goodbye, it
was something of an emotional let-down when the other missionaries left Chek Hom. It was also a profitable time in the
work. The day and evening school had over 500 students; the
Bible Institute had strong national leaders; and the local churches
were growing. It seemed the Lord was preparing the Chinese
people for what lay ahead.

The local church in downtown Chek Hom had called a
national pastor. Pastor Chan graduated from the South China
Bible College in Wuchow, where my parents taught during
World War II.

The refugee church, made up of Christian families from the
village, met in the schoolhouse on Kai Ling on a large piece of
land next to our compound. With the congregation's desire to
own their own house of worship, they started a building fund.
The church would be constructed of mud, straw, and bamboo,
with a tile roof. The church members prayed for a foreman to
supervise the work.

Little Mrs. Leung, with her bound feet, had attended faithfully for more than a year when she came to my mother and said, "My son is dying."

Mother went to Mrs. Leung's mud hut only to find that this grown son was an opium addict. The church began praying for him. Mother cared for him every day, feeding him at first with an eyedropper because he was too weak to eat. After a few months, he was strong enough to walk. He even came to church. He accepted the Lord as his Savior the very first time he heard God's Word. He was hired as the building foreman, an answer to the congregation's prayers in more ways than one.

Bamboo framework staked out the size of the proposed church building. In between the upright poles, a latticework of smaller bamboo was tied into place. A big pile of red clay in the shape of a cone was dumped onto the ground, then numerous buckets of water were poured into the top of the cone. Everyone, including me, used our feet to mix the clay and water into a plaster consistency.

The next step was to take a handful of long straw and lay it on the mud. Then someone picked up the muddy straw, squeezed out the excess mud, and hung it over the bottom horizontal rung of the latticework of bamboo, continuing in this manner until the whole wall was covered with muddy straw. Some areas were left open for the door and windows.

We used a wooden trowel to plaster the whole wall smoothly with a mud-lime mixture which helped keep out termites. When the walls were finished, beams were laid on top to form supports for the slanting tile roof. The final task was to whitewash the whole building. It really looked lovely.

The door was made of two boards with about three inches cut off the top and bottom, leaving a protruding piece that pivoted in a hole at the left and right sides of the doors. These were the hinges on which the doors opened. Each of the doors had its own squeak. I could tell by the door squeak which neighbor was getting up in the morning. The other telltale sign was the tone of their wooden *kecks* as they walked up the dirt path.

By the time the refugee church was dedicated, membership was over 100. Everyone brought their own hand fan for each service, since there was no electricity to keep the members cool. When the pastor looked out across the congregation, he saw a sea of movement.

One of the members was married to a man violently opposed to her being a Christian. The church covenanted together to pray that he would become a Christian. During one Sunday night service, one of the villagers in Kai Ling village reported that her husband had fallen down the village well. His wife went to the site and started preaching to him. She told him he would not be rescued until he received Christ as his Savior. He also had to return to the church that had been praying for him.

Once the man agreed, friends used a rope to get him out. Even though bruised and battered, he staggered into church. There was great rejoicing and thanksgiving. The man became a true believer and later served as a deacon in the church along with the former opium addict. Both of these men developed into great leaders in the church during the time of the communist takeover.

Another incident in the village church occurred during a Wednesday night prayer meeting. Mrs. Lum asked for special prayer that a sow, in which she had invested her life savings, would deliver safely. The sow was overdue.

Mr. Ching asked, "Are you current in your tithing?"

"No," Mrs. Lum answered, "but I will catch up after the piglets are born."

"Aiiee!!" The congregation spoke as one, telling Mrs. Lum that they could not pray for anyone who was short-changing God. Mrs. Lum quickly paid the tithes she had allowed to lapse.

And Sunday morning, after special prayer, 23 piglets were safely delivered.

This village church was strong in faith. Many members joined the group, even after we had to leave. When my parents and I received pictures of the church group in 1950, there were around 125 members.

AN UNEXPECTED TRIP

By September of 1949 the political atmosphere in China had worsened. Father thought it would be a good idea for Mother and me to visit Hong Kong. He probably did not want us around when—not if—the communists came to stay.

Mother and I left Chek Hom on a motorized junk with two large shelves running through the center of the boat to accommodate passengers. The two of us rented a grass mat and rolled it out in the middle of the top shelf for the two days it would take us to sail up the South China Sea to Hong Kong.

Although a mat had been rolled out next to ours, no occupant came to claim it. After dark, an unkempt-looking man dressed in rags laid down beside us. It did not take Mother long to find out that he spoke the Lui Chau dialect, which not many people did that far north. In talking to Mother, the man revealed himself as the extremely rich man who owned the high school on the hill beyond our house. He had to travel in disguise in order to keep from being killed for his money. Only the captain, and now my mother and I, knew his identity.

Bowls of delicious soup were delivered for the three of us. Mother and I were well looked after for the rest of the trip. Mother clearly explained the plan of salvation to our "neighbor," emphasizing that he could reach heaven only by trusting in Jesus Christ as his own personal Savior. *"For by grace are ye saved through faith; and that not of yourselves: it is the gift of God: Not of works, less any man should boast"* (Ephesians 2:8–9).

When our boat entered the harbor in Hong Kong, the

captain announced that we were arriving at a different dock than originally scheduled, once again for our friend's protection. Somehow, he had made sure that the Morgans were notified about this change of arrangements. Mother and I expressed our thanks to him, and the high school owner disappeared. We never saw our neighbor again, but heard that he died soon after our trip. Perhaps we will see him in heaven. At least he knew the way, whether or not he accepted the Lord.

Mother and I checked in at the Sailors and Soldiers Home, where I found a friend named Mary Plymire, an MK from Africa. We had numerous adventures together. The most exciting was when the H.M.S. *Amethyst,* a British gunboat, arrived in Hong Kong after a harrowing experience on the Yangtze River. The most important "person" on that boat was the cat which caught the rats that provided food for the sailors while they were detained by the communists. After many months of being barricaded by huge logs, the British escaped from the blockade.

Mary and I loved to go down by the waterfront and pet the famous cat. The sailors even let us take it for a short walk. On her collar were the gold letters HMS, which stood for His Majesty's Ship. That cat really did serve her king well!

Another pastime Mary and I enjoyed was riding on the Star Ferry that operated between Hong Kong Island and the Kowloon Peninsula. On one occasion, we took the ferry to witness the arrival of a huge luxury liner in Kowloon. The Indian women wore beautiful silk saris with little gold bells on the hems which created a musical serenade as they walked.

As Mary and I stood, entranced, watching the living play unfold in front of us, our friend Mr. Howard Phillips found us and told me, "Everyone is looking for you. You are leaving Hong Kong right away. Your mother read that there's a boat leaving for Tsam Kwan, and she's already on it. You are to go straight back to the Sailors and Soldiers Home."

After a ferry ride back across the harbor, Mary and I rode a streetcar. It went so slowly, we jumped off and ran to catch the one ahead. We were both 13 years old, and full of energy. I cannot imagine doing that today with all the traffic in Hong Kong.

Uncle Jay and a speedy taxi took me to the dock and the boat where my mother waited. With anchor lifted and mooring ropes untied, the steamer ship got under way. This was the same steamer on which Mother and I sailed up the coast, so we rented a grass mat and bedded down for the night as we had done on our way to Hong Kong.

In the morning we found ourselves in Canton. Instead of going down the South China Coast, the steamer sailed up the Pearl River to Canton, where we anchored in the harbor. Mother and I had to hire a sampan to take us to shore. The water was choppy because of an approaching typhoon.

Arriving ashore, Mother and I found the city almost completely deserted. We walked into a big hotel restaurant where only the chef remained. He was surprised we did not know that the communists were expected to arrive and seize the city. Before leaving himself, he fixed us his last egg and some toast. There Mother and I sat in a ritzy hotel, eating our breakfast without another soul in sight!

After breakfast, we cleared our table and walked past the majestic diplomatic buildings into the Chinese part of town. As we walked along, Mother and I heard our names being called. In this city of millions, whom should we meet but Mrs. Lo on her way to the Pui Ling Bible Conference. She said, "Come along. We might as well go to heaven from the conference!"

The preacher spoke on good Queen Vashti from the Book of Esther in the Bible. But as soon as Mother and I heard bullets, we knew we had to hurry back to our boat. The moment we reached the steamer, they pulled up anchor and sailed away, dodging bombs and bullets, and maneuvering in the turbulent water caused by the soon-to-arrive typhoon.

That was not the worst of it; we were headed down the Pearl

River, which had been mined. Only the Lord could keep our boat from hitting the mines we could see bobbing in the water. Out at sea, we had to face the high waves. It took us a week instead of the usual overnight to reach Fort Bayard. When we arrived, we learned the boat before us had its main mast broken off in the typhoon gales.

I had never been so thirsty in my whole life as when Mother and I sat on the customs house doorstep, waiting for Father to come for us. He had arrived at the dock earlier, but was told, "No 'foreign devils' are arriving today." Since it was Sunday, Father drove 10 miles back to Chek Hom for church, and came back to check on us after the service ended. He was a welcome sight!

By the time we made the 10 bumpy miles home, I was extremely ill with a high fever. Even my tongue was swollen from dehydration. Mrs. Wong fed me liquids with an eyedropper and stayed by my bed all night. When I was able to eat again, she fixed me the most delicious chicken soup. Once again, God brought us through what seemed like an impossible situation.

CIRCLE OF FRIENDS

Night after night for 10 nights, from sundown until the temple gong struck 3 a.m., my parents and I (and the entire populace of Kai Ling) were serenaded with wailing in the form of a chant, coming from the other side of the wall.

The reason for this was that Mei Ling, one of my friends from night school, was getting married. According to the dictates of local custom, the bride had to perch on her bed board for 10 days, never touching the ground nor seeing family and friends. This symbolized renouncing her old life to begin a new one. The wailing was to convey to the world her sadness at leaving everything behind.

My friend Lum Kiu and I made a courtesy call. Entering the hut, we were ushered in to the back room where the bride sat cross-legged on her bed behind a grass mat partition. As soon as we entered the room, she immediately began to wail.

When they saw my gift of a flowered cotton handkerchief, her five attendants said that gift was so beautiful that they all had to wail. What a chorus! It lasted for nearly 10 minutes. The young women slept so soundly after the evening of wailing, they said they woke up one morning to find a thief had stolen their covers, and none of them had heard a thing!

Lum Kiu and I were invited to the wedding, held on the tenth—and final—day, when the feasting began. We were told to eat at a certain table in the courtyard where food had not been offered previously to idols. The bride was fed and dressed by her attendants, and now was allowed to step off her bed onto grass mats.

She covered her face with the handkerchief I had given her. Her wedding gown was made of gorgeous embroidered red silk. Her skirt gaped a little, so I ran home to get a safety pin to hold it together. Much to my amazement, it was pinned right in the middle of that elegant gown, in plain sight.

At noon, the wedding parade was ready to start from the village to the top of our hill. Before the bride could leave, she had to receive permission from her older brother by crawling between his legs. He refused to give it because he would now have to do her job of picking up slop for their pigs. This problem was solved by stretching the legs of a pair of his pants above the door for her to walk under, symbolically receiving the permission he had refused to grant.

The attendants led the bride across mats on the ground, moving them to keep her clothes and feet from touching the ground, and holding an umbrella over her to shield her from the sky.

This was a modern wedding because Mei Ling and all her attendants, including Lum Kiu and me, were to be driven to the groom's village by bus. Somehow Mei Ling had found out whom she was to marry, and she would not be secretly carried off in a sedan chair as in the olden days. Her jewelry box with a mirrored top was fixed to the front of the bus. The mirror was believed to ward off evil spirits that lurked in the corners of buildings as we drove through town. The bus reversed and went forward seven times in order to leave the evil spirits behind, according to local Chinese belief.

After a two-mile drive, we arrived at Mei Ling's new home. We had to wait for an hour in the hot bus, attendants fanning the poor girl in her quilted gown. After the groom came out and tapped the bus with his fan, he then tapped his bride. He took her to the temple for the marriage ceremony and feast.

Lum Kiu and I did not stay, as the food served would have been offered first to the idols. We were sad because we would not see Mei Ling for a year, at which time she would be allowed to return to her girlhood home.

When Mei Ling did return, she had an appendicitis attack and nearly died. Mrs. Wong and Mother nursed her back to health, and Mei Ling's family became Christians.

The young people's group drawn from the three churches around Kai Ling, consisted of nine members: four boys and five girls. At 13, I was the youngest. Other members included Lum Kiu and Titus, my old friend. Mother was our director. Once a month, we teens led the Sunday evening church service in Chek Hom.

We met on my front lawn on Wednesdays before prayer meeting to plan and practice. We had many avenues of service such as passing out tracts, helping care for children, setting up benches for the open-air service on Kai Ling, and going through the village ringing hand bells to announce the time for the service. Usually over 500 people attended.

Each member of the youth group had an amazing story. One time while ringing a bell through the village, Su San, one of our group, found no sign of her family. Her father, a French interpreter, was away on business. Neighbors told us that Mrs. So and the baby had died of mushroom poisoning. The two young children were very ill.

I went home and related the story to Mother, who immediately went to the city morgue. Each day, bodies from the morgue that went unclaimed were buried in a common grave. There, searching through the bodies, Mother found Mrs. So and her baby. Mother hired two rickshaws to transport them back up the hill to the Sos' shack. Mother must have been praying hard as she walked beside the rickshaw that transported the dead bodies up Kai Ling. Upon their arrival, Mrs. So was alive, but her baby was dead. It took days for Mother to nurse Mrs. So back to health. The whole family eventually became Christians.

My 14th birthday that year fell on a Sunday, and my party

was held on our front lawn that afternoon. Little did I dream that would be the youth group's last gathering. That evening during the open-air church service, machine guns started their chorus around the city. My father calmly announced that it was a salute in honor of his daughter's 14th birthday, then prudently dismissed the crowd.

twenty • three

PIGS OF PROTECTION

One Sunday afternoon soon after my birthday, a Chinese man named Colonel Chang came to visit my father. The two men sat on our verandah speaking English, as the colonel had been educated in the United States and spoke very good English.

Colonel Chang had been reading modern American novels and brought a list of 16 words that were unfamiliar to him. Since they were not in his dictionary, Col. Chang wanted to know their meanings. My father, being English, was not familiar with American slang. Only one word on the list did he know: "scapegoat."

Father showed Colonel Chang from the Bible the meaning of the word. Christ is our "scapegoat," in that He died to atone for our sins. At this time, Colonel Chang accepted Christ as his personal Savior. Not long afterwards, he brought his mother and a friend, both of whom also became Christians. All three were baptized in our garden baptistery.

Because of the uncertain outcome of the political power struggles, the result was the shooting and scarcity of food. When they went to Hong Kong, the Jenistas left behind a large amount of Gerber's baby food. Each day my parents and I had our choice of junior dinners and puréed fruits or vegetables. There was something comical about the three of us eating baby food.

Mother found boxed puddings and tea among the Jenistas' things. We had expected to take the food with us to Hong Kong, but ended up eating it earlier to keep from starving. When the Jenistas packed their belongings in the United States, they duti-

121

fully tucked mothballs in among their things to keep out bugs. The packaged items absorbed the camphor odor, so my parents and I ate mothball-flavored tea and pudding. We appreciated the "goodies," despite their unappetizing smell.

Colonel Chang reappeared at our house with his senior officer on December 11, 1949. They said, "Even though they've been in and out during the previous year, the communists now are coming for good." At one point, the communist commander left his mother at the downtown church in Chek Hom "for safe-keeping," which put us in an awkward position since we were on the opposite side of the political fence.

Now that the communists were coming to stay, Colonel Chang commandeered a motorized junk to spirit off my parents and me in the early morning. Mrs. Wong, our local Bible woman, was the first to know of our plans, which we had to keep as secret as possible until we made good our escape.

None of us got much sleep that Sunday night! Monday morning, while it was still dark, we packed one suitcase apiece. For breakfast we ate toast with catsup, which was all we had to put on it. Mrs. Wong begged us to leave our dirty dishes on the table. "Cleaning up is a privilege for me," she insisted. She was a godly lady, a great servant of the Lord.

Breakfast would have tasted better if I did not have to get it past the huge lump in my throat. Thinking about leaving home for good was almost unbearable! Somehow I had not given the idea much thought, and it was hard to fathom. My parents and I took comfort from knowing that God was in control, which He certainly was, down to the smallest detail.

As we stood by the compound gate, my dog, Argus, was crying up on the front steps. I ran back up the walk to retrieve my New Testament and to give Argus a final hug. Would I see him again in 20 years like the Argus in Homer's *Odyssey*?

Word had leaked out among the local Christians that my parents and I were leaving Chek Hom. Some stood by the road, tears running down their cheeks, careful not to express their feelings in any other way.

An army truck took the Jenistas' kerosene refrigerator with us to Fort Bayard, 10 miles away. The motorized junk arranged by Colonel Chang was anchored out some distance from the coast. It was already loaded with 400 full-grown pigs in baskets. There also were eight huge baskets, each containing 1,000 eggs packed in straw. When the crated refrigerator was loaded, it almost tipped the boat over. The coolies finally tied it down on top of the cabins.

When it was time to start the boat's engines, nothing happened. We sat in the harbor for two days. Pastor and Mrs. Chen (Di Goo, my former *amah*) sent out food and a present of a rice bowl, chopsticks, and spoon that I still have today.

By Wednesday, half of the city seemed to know a boat was leaving for Hong Kong. Hundreds of people tried to climb on board and sail to safety, out of reach of the communists. When the junk's engine finally did start, many people were pushed off to lighten the load as we left the harbor. All of a sudden, we were pelted with gunfire. What saved our lives were the huge fat pigs, stacked three deep along the rails. They absorbed the bullets intended for us.

What no one knew was that the captain was not licensed to carry passengers, and there were many on-board, hiding among the pigs. Anyone who knows anything about pigs knows their bowel movements are generally stinky diarrhea that runs everywhere. It would have been much worse for all of us if the bullets had not killed three-quarters of the 400 animals.

We did not reach Hong Kong until Saturday night, four days after we left Fort Bayard. The boat floated a good 18 inches below the safe waterline. We arrived safely, only by the grace of God. The captain dropped anchor at Cheung Chau Island, hoping to get rid of his passengers and avoid entering Hong Kong illegally.

The British floodlights at Cheung Chau Island illuminated the filthy mess of our boat. We were towed into Hong Kong as the sun rose over the mountains. Some missionary friends, passing on the Star Ferry, laughed heartily at us. They could see and smell us, which is probably why the customs officers did not bother to come aboard.

Waiting on the dock were Uncle Jay Morgan and ABWE's deuptation director, Rev. Don Moffat, "Uncle Muffin" as we MKs called him. He had been scheduled to pay a visit to Chek Hom. I heard him shout to my father, "Sure glad the commies came. I never could have traveled like that!"

It was hard to believe, but 172 passengers had crammed on that one boat. All of us were lined up, except my father who refused to disembark because he wanted to guard the Jenistas' refrigerator. Also, being English, he had a right to refuse. The rest of us were marched across the main intersection of Nathan Road up to the police station.

Ann Morgan had arrived at the police station with Aunt Dorothy, so we two girls took a stroll. I saw all our fellow travelers huddled in a courtyard, awaiting arrest for illegal entry into Hong Kong. I told my father about their plight, and he went straight to the harbor master's office. Father usually was very calm, but today he was just as riled up as the big boss, who shouted, "We already have too many people in Hong Kong!" The city's population had jumped from 500,000 to three million, with people sleeping on the sidewalks.

"The pigs are needed, but not the people," the harbor master said. That did it. Father pounded on the harbor master's desk for emphasis as he exclaimed, "You mean to tell me that you value pigs over people? We have just experienced a most dangerous journey and are starving. I demand that these 170 people be given a meal and released."

The harbor master honored Father's request as one British subject to another, and the detainees were fed and released.

Now my parents and I needed to find a place to stay. First we stopped at a friend's house and bathed. Then we went to see the Jenistas and their new baby, Carol. With three little ones, the Jenistas were thankful to have their refrigerator back. We were thankful that it arrived safely, and had not rolled into the ocean.

Most hotels were full. The only place that would take us in was the Metropolitan Hotel, the old Philips House. My parents and I were permitted to set up cots in the dining room after dinner, as long as we were out of the way before breakfast. That meant we couldn't go to bed until 11 p.m., and had to get up by 6 a.m. But we were grateful for a place to lay our heads. Anyway, within a week, we had booked passage on a Cunard liner bound for England, or so we thought.

When my father went to check on our travel arrangements, he found that the clerk in the Cunard office had forgotten to sign us up for a cabin. We were back to square one! The Lord had better plans for us. Father found a Dutch freighter, the *Ridderkerk,* leaving for Antwerp, Belgium, in three weeks. That sounded great at this point, as any kind of passage out of Hong Kong was booked up months in advance.

The hotel finally had some vacancies, so my parents got their own room while I shared a room with, of all people, Aunt Faith Snuggs, who used to work with us in South China. On Christmas morning I woke to find a pretty package at the foot of my bed. It contained a beautiful Scottish doll, dressed in the traditional kilt. It remains among my doll collection, thanks to Aunt Faith.

Mr. Blackstone, one of the hotel guests, played a recording of Handel's *Messiah* one evening. We all sat in the dining room enjoying the beautiful music. My parents and I "just happened" to share a table with a doctor, his wife, and 16-year-old son. In the course of conversation, we discovered all of us sailed on the same German ship across the Pacific in 1938. Their son had given me the tricycle ride that almost landed us both in the ocean!

12,000 MILES TO GO:
ASIA

The *Ridderkirk* had been a German raider, a ship built to ram and sink other ships, during World War II. Having three holds for cargo made the ship unusually long; many docks could not accommodate its length.

Father slept down with the crew, while Mother and I shared the pilot's cabin, which opened onto "A" deck. Even the first-class staterooms did not open onto the main deck, and we paid a much lower price because we had bunk beds instead of single beds. We had to sign a paper stating that we would not complain about the food. At least it was edible, more than some things I had eaten in the last few months.

The *Ridderkirk* carried around 20 passengers, including the family of the American ambassador to Japan: his wife; 20-year-old daughter; 15-year-old son, Denny; and nine-year-old daughter, Penny. There were also three Catholic priests and the family of the German ambassador: his wife, 15-year-old daughter, and six-year-old son. The ambassador himself was in a prison camp in Siberia. The family had a hair-raising story of their escape from China. Completing our party were two American journalists and some Dutch businessmen.

Denny, Penny, and I were all getting our education through the Calvert correspondence course. Mother's and my cabin became the ship's classroom, with Mother as teacher. In fact, since Denny and Penny traveled on a single passport, this arrangement made it convenient for them take trips with my family and me to exotic ports. The other family members were not interested. Only in a few ports were the Germans allowed ashore, which did not mean that they were not smuggled ashore by the purser!

MANILA, PHILIPPINES: January 10, 1950

Leaving Hong Kong on January 8, 1950, the *Ridderkirk*'s first stop was Manila. What a contrast to the bombed-out city and the harbor full of sunken ships I had seen in 1946. Only the stern of the *Ridderkirk* could get near the dock, so disembarking took a long time. Father held an ABWE mission meeting with the Philippine missionaries over the rail to save time.

What a welcome when we did step ashore! There was a full house of missionaries at the home of "the Aunties," Millie Crouch and Priscilla Bailey. During that day ashore, Dr. Lincoln Nelson gave us a boat ride around the harbor at night; we ate hand-churned ice cream at the Southeast Asia Broadcasting Company. Dr. Hopewell gave me a beautiful shell, which I still have after more than 50 years. It was around 2 a.m. when my parents and I finally got back to the *Ridderkirk*.

THAILAND: January 16, 1950

Our next stop was Gau See Chung, an island off the coast of Bangkok, Thailand. The *Ridderkirk* was too large to enter the channel and port of Bangkok, so we anchored in the bay and waited to load on two baby elephants destined for Belgium's Antwerp Zoo. We passengers were allowed to go ashore, eight at a time, in a little motorboat shuttle service with sharks following us all the way. The shuttle boat's owner asked where we were from. Father said, "We are the League of Nations."

This island contained the ruins of a 300-year-old palace of the king of Siam, now called Thailand. Talk about a kid's tropical paradise! Denny, Penny, and I explored to our hearts' content. Swimming was great until the sharks decided to join us. The local

Thai people brought us a huge watermelon, which we cut up
with a big shell. Though it was winter, the tropics are always hot,
and we were thirsty.

On another day, we visited a sleepy fishing village. When
Father saw an elderly man sitting in the shade, he started speaking the Lui Chau dialect to him. The old man just came alive! As
a young man he lived just across the Gulf of Tonkin from our
peninsula, and had not heard his native tongue for years. He did
that day, and learned the plan of salvation as well.

Local people were friendly, eager to show off their wares.
One man begged us to come into his hut. There we found a row
of full Coca-Cola® bottles left by American GI's after the war.
Although an inch of dust lay on top of each bottle, we bought
them from him. Even warm Coca-Cola® quenched our thirst.

The cargo we were to load here was rice. It had to be transported to our ship from Bangkok, about 50 miles away. The baby
elephants we were waiting for got the flu, so monkeys were sub-
stituted instead. This completed the ship's mission. Every day
brought exciting places to explore and things to do, and restric-
tions were fewer on a freighter than on a luxury liner.

THE REPUBLIC OF SINGAPORE: January 21, 1950

One of the most interesting places in the world is Singapore,
located one degree north of the equator. Since it was January,
however, the weather was great for us tourists. My parents and I
went ashore Saturday evening to find a church to attend on
Sunday, but the local newspaper carried no listings of churches.

We wandered over to Central Park, where many groups of
people listened to speeches on a variety of topics. One young
man stood on a stump, extolling the virtues (as he saw them) of
communism. It wasn't long before Father had heard enough. He
climbed up on the next stump and challenged the young man,
suggesting he move to Siberia! The young chap suddenly disappeared, and Father preached to his large audience.

We came across a Christian group, singing hymns and giving testimonies. Father asked if he could speak. After being examined by the leader, Mr. Broughton, Father preached a second time. Afterwards Mr. and Mrs. Broughton, C&MA missionaries, invited us to their apartment for tea. During our visit, our host left the room and returned with a missionary named Miss Marsh. This woman had been my mother's classmate at Nyack Bible College in New York back in the early 1920s. What a reunion they had!

On Sunday, Father was invited to speak in the morning at a Chinese church. We ate dinner at a Chinese restaurant, followed by a tour of the Singapore Botanical Gardens. I vividly recall the huge fan palms and the little monkeys, swinging from tree to tree.

PORT SWETTENHAM, MALAYSIA: January 26, 1950

At Port Swettenham, on the coast of Malaysia, the *Ridderkirk* took on iron ore and tons of rubber. Watching from the bridge of our ship, we saw the coolies carrying 200-pound rectangle-shaped chunks of rubber on their backs and dumping them into a big net spread out on the dock. The men had to get away fast, as those heavy chunks bounced like balls.

When the huge crane gathered up the net and swung it up and over to lower it into the hold of the ship, sometimes it hit the deck first and the rubber bounced up like popcorn. A few bounced right into the ocean. Since rubber floats, men dove in to guide the bouyant balls near the dock, where a crane-like machine completed the rescue.

KUALA LUMPUR, MALAYSIA: January 27, 1950

During the time of rubber loading, my parents and I, along with Denny and Penny, took the hour-and-a-half train ride through the jungle and rubber plantations to Kuala Lumpur, Malaysia's capital city. Men worked by the train tracks to keep them clear of jungle vegetation. Monkeys swung from the trees and even came to peek at us through the window glass. Now we were the ones in a zoo!

Kuala Lumpur is a beautiful, modern city. The five of us ate lunch, British-style, in a hotel; each table had to be filled. Since I was seated on the end next to Penny, I asked her to move over so I would not fall off the bench. She whispered, "I can't. There's a machine gun sticking in my side." I lifted up her linen napkin and sure enough, there was a machine gun, resting on the lap of a turbanned man.

We survived lunch, saw more of the city, and enjoyed the train ride back through the jungles to the coast. We were hot, tired, and covered with black cinders from the train's smokestack, but we had a great time. The best part was playing "peek-a-boo" with the monkeys through the train windows.

PENANG, MALAYSIA: January 29, 1950

Sunday found us in Penang visiting Father's friend Pastor Adams. Father was invited to preach in the Cantonese service in his friend's church. Afterwards, a Mr. Cheng treated us all to a delicious Chinese dinner before we toured Penang's Botanical Gardens, every bit as lovely as Singapore's, with the added attraction of beautiful peacocks roaming the rolling hills.

THE INDIAN OCEAN: January 30–February 2, 1950

The longest stretch of sailing still lay ahead: crossing the Indian Ocean to Colombo, Ceylon (now known as Sri Lanka). Denny, Penny, and I found plenty to do besides getting ahead in our schoolwork. Each day we checked the nautical miles we had covered. One stormy day we ventured up to the dining room when no one else dared to. The edges of the dining tables were up to keep everything from rolling over the sides of the tables, and the tablecloths were wet to keep the plates from sliding off. The menu of macaroni and cheese was guaranteed to stick to the plate, and one of our favorite meals to boot.

The most fun was that the chairs had wheels on them, and each time the ship rolled, we children tried to see which of us could get his chair back to the wall first. Rolling back into place, we grabbed a few bites before making the return trip. Then we got the idea to roll our three chairs out on the enclosed bridge below the captain's bridge. There were no obstructions, and we raced to our hearts' content. When we "older" two tired out, Penny wound up the old gramophone and entertained us with beautiful ballet performances.

COLOMBO, CEYLON: February 3, 1950

A lovely, sunny—but silent—day greeted us at Colombo. Nothing and no one stirred. We learned that the harbor was closed because an elaborate parade honoring Buddha was about to take place. Fortunately for us, the pilot boat agreed to take us ashore. Mother and I were dressed up in matching outfits we made on-board ship after leaving Hong Kong.

First, the dancers in their exotic costumes paraded by. Then we found ourselves less than 10 feet from an elephant bedecked with silver filigree and a beautiful embroidered silk draping. On its back sat a gold urn about three-feet tall, supposedly containing a tooth of Buddha. This tooth of Buddha was a gift from Ceylon being transported to a temple in Thailand. This was definitely a once-in-a-lifetime event to behold.

My parents had arranged to meet Mr. Alfred Abayakoon. He arrived with a bouquet of flowers for Mother. I remember how handsome this tall, dark-skinned man looked in his white suit. He drove us all around the island and gave Father a report of the ABWE work there. After dinner my parents and I returned to our ship, still marveling at what the Lord had prepared for us that unforgettable day. The bouquet of gladiolas Mr. Abayakoon brought was not only a thoughtful gesture, it also added a touch of spring to our cabin.

THE MIDDLE EAST

ADEN, SOUTH YEMEN: February 9, 1950

The *Riddenkirk* docked at Aden, at the mouth of the Red Sea. What a contrast to beautiful green Colombo! Here, we were told, no rain had fallen for seven years. Everyone carried his own cup in order to buy water from the camel cart. Anyone who owned a camel, cart, and a drum with a spigot could set himself up in business—if only water could be found. Imagine not being able to take a bath or wash clothes for years!

Our sightseeing took us to huge cisterns, reported to have been built by King Solomon and the Queen of Sheba. Peering down into one of them, a grown man appeared no bigger than a toy. There was just a little puddle of water, probably from a spring, in the otherwise empty cistern. We walked down the winding steps all the way to the bottom. It was like being in a huge canyon.

Much preparation had been made for the next stop: Egypt. Mother sent Denny, Penny, and me on a journey back in time. Denny and Penny heard the story of Joseph in Egypt, and how God preserved the Jewish nation. We gleaned much from our school history books, and made lists of what we wanted to see in the Cairo Museum and elsewhere.

In the meantime, we were sailing up the Red Sea, so named because as the sun sets, the reflection gives the sea and mountains a red hue. Early the next morning, we all piled out on deck in our pajamas to watch the sun rise over the Sinai Peninsula.

SUEZ, EGYPT: February 13, 1950

We were anxious to get going when we dropped anchor at Suez. A Cook's Tour, advertised at only U.S. $50 for the journey from Suez to Cairo and on to Port Said, seemed too good to pass up. Limos waited to take us on the two-and-a-half-hour drive across the desert.

We waited and waited, and waited some more. After about two hours, the Egyptian customs commissioner at Suez ushered my father into another room and asked confidentially, "What are greenbacks?"

The two American reporters had declared their money as "greenbacks." Frantic phone calls and dictionaries did not reveal the meaning of this perplexing word. I guess the officials felt more comfortable asking an Englishman than in showing their ignorance to American reporters. Once they understood the nickname for U.S. currency, we were on our way. Although the road was paved, it felt like we were driving through a sea of sand which, in effect, we were!

CAIRO, EGYPT: February 14, 1950

By midnight on the 13th, we were all in bed at the Victoria Hotel after a quick tour of the lights of Cairo, the capital city of Egypt. Our 4 a.m. wake-up call on Valentine's Day came all too soon. The limousine waited to drive us eight miles to Giza. Yet how many times does anyone have the opportunity to see a sunrise over the pyramids?

Wow! What a heap of rocks! Each "stone" is about seven feet high and weighs an average of two-and-a-half tons. The Great Pyramid, considered one of the seven wonders of the ancient world, covers about 13 acres, which is greater than the area of 11 football fields.

We rode camels across the desert past two other pyramids to see the Sphinx. Penny and I doubled up in the saddle of a single camel. Our camel stopped on a cliff above the Sphinx, and our camel driver tried to make the beast sit down. The camel had different ideas. He kept turning his head around and looking us in the eye, hissing, and showing his rotten teeth. Maybe he did not want to get up that early in the morning either.

A camel sits down in stages: back legs first, then front legs. Our camel driver kept whipping the camel's leg until he finally bent his hind legs. Penny and I nearly fell off backwards. After a few more whippings, the camel bent his front knees and we hung on for dear life, as the cliff was right in front of us and it seemed as if we were going to pitch forward onto the Sphinx. When the camel finally settled all the way down, we girls were relieved to be able to climb off! The Sphinx appeared majestic and immovable, all 240 feet of it, sitting on its stone platform in the desert sand as it has done for more than 4,000 years.

Back at the Great Pyramid, we looked out over Cairo as our guide pointed out historical landmarks. It was hard to imagine this area's rich history over the previous 5,000 years. There was so much to see and absorb; it was mind-boggling.

After a limousine ride through the city, we arrived at the world-famous Cairo Museum, where Cook's Tours allotted us one hour. Since we three children had our own list of things to see, we went off on our own. We started on the top floor, where we hit a "gold mine." No one was there except a curator, who expressed interest in our list.

He showed us chariots that Moses might have ridden in. He even let us each stand on one. On the same floor were four huge gold-covered boxes, each one a little smaller so that they nested inside each other, sliding in from different directions. This was to make it more difficult for thieves to reach the sarcophagus housed inside the smallest box, where the jewels and mummy were entombed.

Our school history book had told about Cheops, builder of the Great Pyramid, and the archaeologists' discovery of his mother's tomb. A room full of items from her tomb were set up as they had been found. It contained a four-poster bed, among many other things, but what we really wanted to see was Cheops' mother's pure gold fingernail file. A guide told us, "No such object exists." But we children refused to take "no" for an answer. You can imagine our excitement when we spotted it in a glass cabinet, shaped just like the nail files used today, proving the proverb, "There is nothing new under the sun."

Reluctantly leaving the Cairo Museum, we drove to a bazaar. There we saw how beautiful patterns were tapped out in brass. We could have spent hours admiring all the exotic items for sale, but we had just enough time left to visit a huge mosque. We had to remove our shoes and put on cloth slippers before entering. There were no chairs to sit on during worship, only huge Persian rugs on which the men knelt, while the women remained sequestered behind a screen at the rear, separated from the men.

PORT SAID, EGYPT: February 14, 1950

It was time to board the train to Port Said. While we were all drinking in the sights of the Old World, the *Ridderkirk* was wedged sideways in the Suez Canal. Naval law says that if a ship is still immovable after 24 hours, it is blown up in order to clear the passage for international shipping. After the 23-hour mark passed, the *Ridderkirk* was set free. It was by the dock at Port Said, waiting for us when we arrived.

ALEXANDRIA, EGYPT: February 15, 1950

The next unexpected stop was both wonderful and terrifying! We sailed west off the coast of Egypt and, at midnight, dropped anchor in the harbor of Alexandria, where my father had dedicated his life to the Lord while in the Royal Air Force. We could see King Farouk's palace lit up against the night sky. Our ship was scheduled to load cargo. That meant we passengers could spend the next day ashore.

The calm sea grew choppy in the morning and, since the

only way to town was by sailboat, my mother chose to stay on-board ship. Smart lady, for it was one of the scariest rides I have ever experienced, zig-zagging in a sailboat across the harbor, try-ing to catch the right wind without tipping over. Solid land under our feet felt just fine!

We went "from the frying pan into the fire." All of us were excited to visit the catacombs, underground passageways where Christians lived during the persecution of the early church. We understood the law, "NO PICTURES ALLOWED," but one of the American reporters decided to sneak a picture. We were down in the catacombs when we heard a yelling crowd which started hurling stones. The police came to our rescue and we left that area in a hurry.

Father took me on a bus ride, pointing out the building that housed the teahouse where he met Marjory Mitchell. She is the person who led him to the Lord, and the woman for whom my parents named me.

At sunset, we all met back on the dock to hire a water taxi, preferably a motorboat this time. The boatsmen pretended not to speak English; they knew we had to return to our ship and wanted to get the highest possible price they could from us.

While the adults grappled with the water taxi boatmen, Denny, Penny, and I spotted a dim light in a nearby building. I cringe now to think how we groped our way to this place in the dark. Somehow we had the courage to interrupt a group of men, perhaps even the harbor master, to ask for help. They accompa-nied us, flashlights in hand, and took charge of the situation. We were ever so thankful to be back on-board ship. You might say it was an educational experience.

THE CONTINENT

MEDITERRANEAN SEA: February 16, 1950

We enjoyed smooth sailing through the Mediterranean Sea, a dirty green color and not as deep as other large bodies of water. Can you imagine all the sunken treasure that lay hidden in it from the thousands of years of shipping? We also thought about Paul's missionary journeys and hoped the sea would remain calm for us.

By the 18th of February, we neared the Straits of Messina, where the toe of Italy looks as if it is kicking Sicily two miles away. Mount Etna, the famous volcano, was dormant when we passed Sicily. In ancient times, thousands of people lost their lives when this volcano erupted; now, only smoke columns show where the volcano lay.

At dark, we stood on deck to witness the gigantic fireworks of the Stromboli Volcano, north of Sicily on the Lipary Islands. Ribbons of molten lava flowed down its sides. Although we were miles away, the volcano certainly put on a spectacular show for us.

As we sailed up the coast of Italy, we went near a little island called Elba, where Napoleon was exiled, supposedly never to be heard from again. I will never forget the title of the chapter about Napoleon in my 4th grade history book, quoting the statement Napoleon supposedly made (in English of course) in 1814: "ABLE WAS I ERE I SAW ELBA," and arguably one of the world's most famous palindromes Hold the statement up to a mirror.

You see, after a year of exile, Napoleon felt like he could conquer the world. He returned to power for a mere 100 days before suffering terrible defeat at Waterloo, forcing him to abdicate and surrender to the British.

GENOA, ITALY: February 20, 1950

In the early morning, we glimpsed the lights of Genoa, birthplace of Christopher Columbus. This was a bittersweet time, as Denny and Penny were leaving us to meet their father, Ambassador Hodge, in Rome for the 1950 Holy Year.

Denny and Penny had become like family members. We three studied our lessons together every day. They loved to join my parents and me in singing and playing games, especially Sorry® and Scrabble®. I hope to see those two siblings again someday.

On our last day together, everyone had their heart set on eating an authentic Italian spaghetti dinner. With the Catholic priests as our guides, we arrived in a little alley where they asked a man standing in a doorway if he could provide a real Italian spaghetti dinner for twelve. He sad, *"Va bene!"* (Okay!) He told us to come back in an hour, so off we went to see the sights.

The priests took us to a cathedral to see a famous stained-glass window. During World War II it had been dismantled piece by piece and stored in an underground vault in case the church was bombed. The colorful window measured at least 12 feet or more in diameter. The carvings and the rest of the interior of the cathedral were gorgeous. I could not help but wonder how much of God's Word was preached there; it looked more like a museum than an active house of worship.

We asked a policeman directions to Columbus' house but he did not know. He even told us, "Columbus never lived in Genoa." Once again, we three children were not going to take "no" for an answer. We walked blocks, and there it was, a skinny old building standing by itself and looking just like the picture in our history book. The sad part was that we missed seeing the inside by about ten minutes! At least we got to take pictures of the exterior. On the way back to our much-anticipated dinner, we stopped to tell that policeman where the famous landmark was located. He acted surprised that it existed.

When we arrived back at the little alley place, the tables were set outside with red-checked tablecloths. What a feast! It was a memorable ending to 44 remarkable days of camaraderie. We had traveled thousands of miles and seen many wonders of the world, making important memories for a lifetime. We said goodbye to Denny, Penny, and the rest of their family before returning to the *Ridderkirk* to sail for France.

MARSEILLES, FRANCE: February 21, 1950

What I remember most about Marseilles are the wide boulevards. It seemed such a long way across the streets. Although the buildings were majestic, the city itself was dirty. While window-shopping, I spied a little silver cicada brooch, which my parents purchased for me. The cicadas were the little creatures I put inside my mosquito net at night in South China to wake me up when they "sang" in the morning. I still have the brooch, and occasionally wear it to the school where I teach. My students often enjoy reading about this unique little creature.

Back in the 1950s, before a ship sailed, a vendor sold collectors' stamps on the dock. Whenever my parents and I visted a new country, U.S. currency had to be exchanged for that country's money. This transaction could be completed in the ship's purser's office before we disembarked for town. We usually had some change left when returning to the ship, so I was allowed to spend it on stamps. Because of this practice, my stamp collection thrived in size and variety. Denny, Penny, and I traded stamps once a week; we all had beautiful stamp albums.

ROCK OF GIBRALTAR: February 24, 1950

Around noon we got our first glimpse of the famed Rock. What a magnificent sight! The Strait of Gibraltar separates Europe from Africa, a distance of about 10 miles, and the Rock itself marks the point where the Mediterranean Sea meets the Atlantic Ocean.

Sailing up the coast of Portugal, the *Ridderkirk* reached the Bay of Biscay, north of Spain and west of France. The bay is notorious for its storms. Our huge ship was like a toothpick bobbing and rolling as she tried to make her way north. We all stayed in our cabins. The view from the porthole looked like mountains of water on either side with our ship in the valley. This terrible roiling sea lasted for two days.

The first day I ventured upstairs for a macaroni lunch. A couple of us brave (or foolish) souls stood, trying to grab a bit and hold on at the same time. One such experience was enough for me. It was scary just getting back to my cabin door. The weather report said: "Heavy swell, moderate sea." What would a "heavy sea" have looked like? I'm glad I did not have to find out.

The following day was much better as we rounded the coast of France, sailed past the Channel Islands, and headed up the English Channel.

At this point I wondered how the 131 tall sailing ships of the Spanish Armada in 1588 ever reached the English Channel. They must have been great sailing ships to navigate through the Bay of Biscay, but did not do their homework to find out how narrow the Channel was. That must have been quite a sight!

It did not disturb Sir Francis Drake, who was in the middle of a bowling game when he received the news of the fleet's arrival. He is reported to have said, "Let us finish our game. There will still be time to beat the Spaniards."

ANTWERP, BELGIUM: February 28, 1950

After traveling through the English Channel we entered the Strait of Dover, the body of water separating England from

Left:
Steps of temple

Below:
Jay and Dorothy Morgan and Marjory in front of the Chek Hom church

ni, the English interpreter, and
mother, a doctor

Above:
Marjory and David Miller arrive at Fort Bayard, December 27 1985

Left:
Time to feast

Returning to visit Marjory's first home in Lui Chau City where she lived for two years

Left to right: Wing Lok Lo, David and Marjory Miller, Uncle Jay Morgan, Chee Kwun, Aunt Dorothy Morgan, and Mrs. Lo

Above:
Marjory reunited with old friends in China, 1985

Left:
Marjory with Saw Hop Ja (the servant Margaret Barnett trained for the Jenistas in 1949), ca. 1985

The grapevine Dad Barnett planted in 1940

arjory and David Miller with Mini on
shopping spree in China, 1985

Above:
Marjory and Di Goo

Left:
David Miller in temple
moon gate at Lake
Surprise

Left:
David and Tina Miller

Below:
Kathy, Andrew, James, and Kurt VanderWeide

France, 21 miles wide at its narrowest point. About 70 miles northeast we came to the Scheldt River, which flows between Belgium and the Netherlands. The *Ridderkirk* sailed up this river to Antwerp. It took several hours to reach the port, as we had to go through several sets of locks. With the *Ridderkirk* being so long, the captain had to nose in on an angle. It took some maneuvering to get the ship through.

Once safely in port and docked, my parents and I were pleased to see Miss Esther Hoyt, a fellow missionary from Wealthy Street Baptist Church in Grand Rapids. She and Miss Lou Summers, also from the church in Grand Rapids, worked with the Belgium Gospel Mission. Aunt Esther drove us the 30 miles to Brussels, the capital of Belgium.

BRUSSELS, BELGIUM: February 28, 1950

Brussels is famous for its lace, tapestries, and carpets, among other things. The best part about Brussels, for me, was seeing Aunt Lou Summers. As an MK, I was blessed to have many "aunts" and "uncles" all around the world. Aunt Lou took my parents and me sightseeing.

Aunt Lou was in charge of providing the meals for a Bible school connected with the Belgium Gospel Mission. Beef was expensive, but she was able to purchase some inexpensive roasts for one special dinner.

A week later, Aunt Esther asked, "When can we have a delicious beef roast again?"

Aunt Lou clarified, "You mean the horse meat?"

Aunt Esther got sick just thinking about what she'd eaten in cheerful ignorance.

My parents and I ate breakfast and supper with the Aunties in their apartment, and our main meal with the Bible school students. We could sit with students speaking one of any of the following languages: French, Spanish, Italian, Dutch, Flemish, or English. Aunt Lou and Aunt Esther spoke all those languages.

During our four days in Belgium, my parents and I saw the

Congo Museum, a beautiful cathedral, Belgium Art Gallery, and many other sights. My favorite was the art gallery, which housed beautiful works by famous Flemish artists: Van Dyck, Rubens, and Van Gogh, to name a few. A huge painting of the Crucifixion of Christ hung in a room by itself. Viewers had to stand across the room in order to take in all the details.

The next day my parents and I rode the train to Oostende, Belgium. A ferryboat took us past the famed "white cliffs of Dover" to England, where we boarded a train to London.

HOME COUNTRIES:
ENGLAND AND
THE UNITED STATES

LONDON, ENGLAND: March 3, 1950

The day after we arrived in London, Father and I went to check on the new car we had purchased in Hong Kong, to take delivery in London. The car dealership needed a few days to finish readying the new automobile. Imagine owning a new vehicle! Cars were scarce then, and ours was the only one in the showroom. We were grateful to the Lord for our wonderful new car.

At the opening of Parliament on March 6, my parents and I watched the royal parade, gold coaches and all. It didn't even rain, which is rare for London.

One day while we were out shopping, Queen Elizabeth and Prince Philip drove by in an open landau, despite the terrible weather. The evening paper told about a man who ran into the corner of a building and broke his nose that morning. Now that is heavy fog!

We checked on boat tickets and how to ship our car to the United States. We also finished shopping. I particularly liked riding the big double-decker buses, except when two buses passed each other in an intersection. It seemed they would certainly crash. But, thanks to the skill of the bus drivers, that never happened; at least, not while I was riding.

Wednesday was the highlight of our time in London. We met my father's brother, Bert, and his family under the famous Marble Arch. It was fun to get acquainted with my Uncle Bert, Aunt Alice, and three cousins, John, Peter, and Pam (exactly my age). Now I knew at least five of my English relatives.

When my parents and I returned to our hotel, the lobby was packed with people. As we tried to squeeze our way up the big staircase, we looked down to see a little box-like thing flickering with greenish pictures. Television had arrived in London!

The day had come to take possession of our new car and leave London. We peeked through the showroom window before we entered, admiring the grey Standard Vanguard. What a beauty! A man standing inside, also admiring our new car, told us that his name had been on an order waiting list for five years. By purchasing our car in Hong Kong, we had no wait and paid one-third less in the bargain.

The salesman took Father for a ride to show him all he needed to know about driving the new car. The most difficult aspect was that this car was built for export, with the steering wheel on the opposite side, which meant passing cars "blind." Mother acted as Father's navigator, and somehow we made it safely to Wiltshire, 80 miles away.

We spent almost six wonderful months in England, traveling all over. The week we spent in the beautiful Lake District at the Keswick Convention was unforgettable. Dr. Graham Scroggie, one of the speakers, in his eighties, told about his first visit to the convention over 50 years earlier.

He had saved up money for a long time and arrived by train, only to find there were no rooms left. A kind lady gave him a blanket to lay on in her attic. When he awoke, the sun was up and he could hear 5,000 people in the big tent singing the theme song, "Full salvation, full salvation . . ." He just knew that he was in heaven. Then he raised up and bumped his head on the rafters, and he knew he was not in heaven.

While my parents and I attended the convention, we made afternoon side trips to sights such as the home of the poet William Wordsworth and other historical places of interest.

On July 28 my parents and I sailed from Liverpool on the Cunard liner, the *Georgic*. Many friends and relatives saw us off. One special friend, Mr. Matthews, a man in his eighties whom we met in the little village of Edgeworth where my father was born, came all the way down to see us off.

When I said "goodbye" to Mr. Matthews, he replied, "My head is like heaven; there's no parting there." (He was totally bald.) His comment injected a little humor into an otherwise somber group saying farewell to one another.

A big ship on the ocean is an awesome place to be. There is only sky and water as far as the eye can see, and that magical horizon where they meet. Before we sighted land, we would begin to see a few seagulls. The birds let us know we were only a few miles from land.

Halifax, Nova Scotia, was the *Georgic*'s last stop, to unload and load more passengers. Then we were off to see the Statue of Liberty. Little did I know that my third grade class, 47 years later, would win a national Elmer's Glue contest by reconstructing a scale model replica of the famed Lady Liberty, using Elmer's products. Our handiwork is still on display in the library of Glenwood Elementary School in Kentwood, Michigan.

NEW YORK CITY, USA: August 6, 1950
There is nothing like arriving in New York City and first laying eyes on the Statue of Liberty. So many rushed to starboard that the captain had to tell us to divide up, because the ship was listing.

A Roman Catholic missionary nun from Africa stood at the rail with my parents and me. This was her first time back to the United States in 25 years, and would be her only furlough. She would return to Africa to serve there for the rest of her life. When she left us, she said, "See you in heaven."

NORTH QUINCY, MASSACHUSETTS: August 7, 1950

A train took us to Boston's South Station where we caught a taxi to North Quincy, my grandparents' hometown. My grandmother was in the midst of baking bread, and did it smell good! The house had been remodeled, so I now had a room of my own up in the attic. My grandmother had made curtains and a bedspread with appliqued butterflies on them. There were even butterflies on the furniture. It was really my room, and we were finally HOME!

CULTURE SHOCK

At age 14, I was only halfway through the Calvert Correspondence Course's fifth grade. I fell behind because most of my early schooling was in Chinese, and during the war years, disruptions were more constant than schooling. Added to all of that was the mix-up in my birth registration. In order to obtain American citizenship, I was required to reside in the United States from age 16 to 21. What a mess!

I hope missionaries today are better trained in planning for a family overseas. My parents felt that, in all things, "The Lord will provide." He certainly did, but a lot of grief could have been avoided with a little planning. My own thoughts are: the Lord comes first, family next, and work of any kind is last. After all, especially on the mission field, the first "Bible" local people read is how well the missionary family practices what it preaches.

My parents planned to return to South China in July of 1951, so they decided to enroll me in Wheaton Academy. Since the school started with the ninth grade, I had some quick catching up to do. Unbeknownst to me, Mother went to North Quincy Junior High School and enrolled me in the eighth grade. Apparently the officials there went by my age in accepting me, no questions asked. All I know was that studies took priority in my life from that moment on.

One nice thing about home schooling is that it offers freedom to go places. My Uncle Bob owned an island in Moss Lake on Cape Cod. With my schoolbooks in hand, we spent a memorable week on the Cape.

September came all too soon. I went off to junior high school, about six blocks from home. On the way, I passed by the homestead of John Quincy Adams, America's fourth president and the man for whom the town of Quincy is named.

In my school of over 1,000 students, I was the only student who had braids, no joke. That wasn't the only difference between me and the other students. I followed the crowd from homeroom each morning to different classrooms for each subject. While this is a typical experience for most junior high students in the United States, it was completely bewildering to someone like me, who'd only ever sat in one room for school.

In history, the teacher asked, "What is the name of the longest *bidge* over the Mississippi?"

I could not figure out the answer he wanted. Because I could not understand him, he broke his yardstick over my desk. When he pointed to the picture, I had the answer: "Huey Long." I didn't realize that New Englanders drop their "r's" when they speak, so when he asked about the longest *bidge,* the history teacher really wanted to know the name of the longest *bridge.*

I could barely read, and did not know what to do during library hour. Most of the time I was pretty good at faking my way through anything, but this one stumped me. I sat at a back table and put my head down, not realizing my class had returned to homeroom. Bless her heart, a kind librarian found me. When she discovered I was from China, she had just the book for me: *A Girl Without a Country* by Margaret Sangster.

I will never forget this story about an American girl my age who had gotten separated from her diplomat father during World War II. She traveled over some of the same roads I had in China. The small book was easy to read. I must have read it six times, improving my reading skills each time. At least it helped to take away the fear I had of reading. It also gave me the idea that maybe someday I could write a book about my travels. You never know what a little act of kindness might bring forth in years to come.

With fifth grade studies at night and so much to learn culturewise during the day, I had no time to feel sorry for myself. Actually I thought everyone else had the same difficult schedule I did.

Included in the eighth grade curriculum at North Quincy Junior High School was an IQ test, where I earned a score of 29. That brought many curious teachers flocking around to see what a student with such a score looked like. My mother was called in to a conference with Mrs. Neely, the school counselor.

I heard her tell my mother, "Do not expect your daughter to be able to advance past the eighth grade."

On the way home I asked Mother, "What did Mrs. Neely mean?"

She replied, "Mrs. Neely was talking through her hat."

I puzzled over Mother's answer for years. How could Mrs. Neely talk through her hat when she hadn't even worn a hat? It was a blessing that I did not understand what Mrs. Neely was saying about my (supposed) lack of intellect.

My parents and I began attending North Quincy Baptist Church. We had been going for some time when my father needed the pastor to sign some documents. One Sunday between Sunday school and church, Father asked the pastor if he would sign the documents. The pastor welcomed us and said he hoped we would come again. My father stunned the pastor by explaining that we had been attending for several months.

During the morning service, the pastor related to the congregation what had just happened. He was so broken over the coldness of his church, the pastor asked my father to come up to the pulpit and speak. Father did. They became a very friendly congregation.

Later I met a girl at school, Amy, who attended that church. Amy invited me to Pioneer Girls, which proved to be a wonderful experience! It takes a lot of hard work to be accepted, no matter what a person's age. Churches should be warm and inviting, but sometimes they are ice-cold to strangers.

The music teacher at my junior high school had talked to us students about learning to play instruments. I told her that my grandfather played a violin and I wanted to learn. After the school concert one night in January, my teacher walked right over to my parents and said that I was interested in learning to play the violin. I was so excited!

My mother said, "That won't be possible."

I can't believe I did this, because my mother didn't believe a child should ever question her parents, but I asked right there, "Why?"

Mother said, "I'll tell you later."

I knew better than to bring up the subject again, but I soon found out the answer.

Arriving home from school the next day, I found the *Esse,* a yearbook from Hampden DuBose Academy, lying on the table. It was opened to a picture of Jaymes Morgan, with whom I grew up in China.

My mother asked, "Would you like to go and see Jaymes?"

Of course I said, "Yes."

"Good," she replied, "because we are going next week."

That was my preparation for boarding school. I did not know when or why my parents' plans had changed—I had thought I would be attending Wheaton Academy—and didn't discover the reason for many years. Leaving the cold northeast sounded good to me, but it did not dawn on me that I was going to Florida for the next four-and-a-half years. It was all so mind boggling.

Jaymes was there to welcome me. I cannot begin to express my feelings at that time. Talk about culture shock! I was thankful my mother had the presence of mind to cut my hair before I went to boarding school so I wasn't still sporting long braids. I met three other MKs who had been born in Matilda Hospital in Hong Kong, as I had.

It seemed as if I had been catapulted from a mud hut to a palace. Dr. DuBose was an MK from China, who appeared both warm and friendly. His wife, however, appeared just the opposite. In her many hours of lecturing, she was skilled in belittling others. How I ever ended up staying at the academy, only God knows. I guess He knew I needed the discipline that Hampden DuBose offered.

I thrived on the regimen, but every time I turned around I faced another bewildering unknown. What was a Valentine's party? I had no idea. Then I was told that I would have to wear a formal to this party. One was lent to me, but you can imagine how I felt wearing borrowed finery.

Something new hit me almost every day. I just had to roll with the punches, because the last thing my father said to me was, "If you ever have to leave here, I would have to come home, and that would be a waste of the Lord's money." In my darkest hours, the Lord became the most real to me.

I admonish missions and churches to get involved, both by prayer and physically, in the lives of missionaries' children left behind. Four years passed before anyone visited me at Hampden DuBose Academy. The Cederlunds, from Grand Rapids, took me out to dinner. That forged a bond which later led to them becoming like my adoptive parents.

The Christian and Missionary Alliance realized the potential of investing in their missionary children. Every year, Dr. Snead, the C&MA president, came down to spend time with their missionary kids. He met with the whole group, then with siblings, and then with each one individually. With that kind of backing, those MKs received more respect. The school knew that they had to answer to the C&MA's advocate in to regard their MKs' welfare.

Out of an average student body of 200, about 20% came from foreign countries. Most of those students were MKs. The missionary kids were the backbone of the school; thus, we really got the most out of it. We usually held the top honors and the most responsible jobs.

Every student had a chore, whether sweeping a sidewalk or working kitchen duty, cleaning guestrooms, keeping up the grounds, or tending the horses and chickens. The work assignment changed every two weeks. I held almost every job during the course of my four-and-a-half years at the academy. The chores taught me the benefits of organization, discipline, and hard work.

Hampden DuBose Academy was really an elite finishing school with a spiritual emphasis which came from the faculty. They dedicated their lives to training young people without monetary reimbursement. We alumni now realize that we would not be the people we are today if it were not for these godly instructors. I hold them in high esteem, and thank the Lord that I had the privilege to study under them. Many have gone on to be with the Lord, but for those still living, it is a joy to acknowledge their godly commitment. Thanks and love to Miss Anderson, my Bible teacher, who gave us all a good foundation in God's Word; to Mrs. Cole, my speech teacher; Mrs. Glatfelter, my algebra teacher; Miss Hill, who taught history; Miss Lawrence, the physical education teacher; and Miss Stone, the English instructor.

At the baccalaureate service in my senior year of high school in 1955, the guest speaker was Dr. Wade McCargo. My father was on the platform to lead in prayer. Dr. McCargo said that he did not feel worthy to be on that platform. "Because of a certain person's testimony and commitment to God, my own life had been changed," Dr. McCargo said. He pointed to my father, saying, "When asked to transfer mission fields, Rev. Barnett said, 'The Lord called me to China. Even if it should cost me my life, I will return!'"

Dr. McCargo had attended the ABWE mission board meeting in Philadelphia when my parents were asked to transfer to the

Philippines, since China seemed to be closed. When my father disagreed, the mission board asked them instead to begin the ABWE work in Hong Kong. It was at this time my parents learned they needed to remain in the United States until I entered boarding school. I couldn't attend Wheaton Academy, since it had no eighth grade. That's how I came to be a student at Hampden DuBose Academy.

Dr. McCargo went on to tell how he called Dr. DuBose in Florida to say, "You're getting a new student."

Dr. DuBose protested, "But we're full; we have no extra beds."

Dr. McCargo persisted, "Then go buy a cot. Marjory Barnett will be there for the second semester of eighth grade!"

You can imagine my surprise that morning when I heard how the Lord had worked out all those details. It helped to explain why I made it through those four-and-a-half years: it was part of God's plan for my life.

Hampden DuBose Academy operated as a boarding school for 50 years, before closing. It reopened as a day school under the capable leadership of Mr. and Mrs. George DuBose, grandson of the founder.

GROWING UP
WESTERN STYLE

My high school graduation in 1955 was traumatic. When my parents arrived after a four-and-a-half-year absence, I hardly knew them. I am sure they felt the same about me. They had left me in bobby socks and now I was all dressed up wearing high heels.

After Dr. McCargo's baccalaureate message, my parents were invited to the academy's guest table for Sunday dinner. Just before we left the campus, Mrs. DuBose had a final stern lecture for my parents; missionaries were not her favorite guests.

My parents and I left Florida for Wheaton, Illinois, to attend Jaymes Morgan's graduation. Then we went to Grand Rapids for a "Welcome Home" at Wealthy Street Baptist Church. We stayed with John and Louise Cederlund, who soon became my second parents. Now the future did not seem so scary and uncertain. I felt like I had an anchor in the Cederlunds.

A return visit to North Quincy was our next stop. This time I had my own familiar room, and some old friends to see. It was there that I received my acceptance to The King's College in New York. The strange thing was that I had never applied. My roommate at Hampden DuBose Academy was the vice president's daughter, and she had sent in my application. That's one way to get students! From then on, I never filled out an application form, whether for nursing school, college, or employment.

Did I "just happen" to be in the right place at the right time? No, God led me, every step of the way.

Two weeks before I was to enter The King's College, my mother and I rode the train into Boston to buy me a suit. We found a nice gray one for $7, and also saw a nice fall dress. But Mother said we had only asked the Lord for a suit, so we would have to pray about the dress. The next day, when she went to Boston by herself, the dress was still there. She bought it for $5. I wore those two outfits for years.

When Mother returned from Boston, her arrival coincided with a telegram from the Cederlunds. They wanted me to take the Thursday train to Grand Rapids to visit them for Labor Day weekend. Mother didn't want me to go because we had just been there, but Father said this was of the Lord and I should go.

That night another telegram from the Cederlunds requested that I come a day earlier, on Wednesday. So the next morning I was Grand Rapids bound. Later we read that the Thursday train had derailed and gone into the river in Connecticut, with many casualties.

During my six days with the Cederlunds, I was the most relaxed that I had ever been in my life. The reason the Cederlunds wanted me in Michigan was to buy my college wardrobe. I had not even thought of needing a winter coat! The Cederlunds provided more than I needed. The Lord knew my needs and supplied them all. It was during this visit I found out that the Cederlunds, who had no children of their own, had paid through ABWE for my education at Hampden DuBose Academy. Even my parents did not know whom the Lord was using to supply those funds.

I attended The King's College during the school's first year at the Briarcliff Manor campus. It had been a fancy hotel at the turn of the 20th century, and the location overlooking the Hudson was gorgeous. Mary Esther, from Hampden DuBose Academy, was my roommate. Another classmate whom I have kept in touch with is Millie Copeland, a teacher at Faith Academy in the Philippines for more than 30 years. Friendships are a priceless possession!

In January, I became ill, so the Cederlunds asked me to live with them. Soon after arriving in Grand Rapids, I heard about a practical nursing course. I went to apply, but was asked to take the regular RN course. I showed up for the one-year course and was allowed in. When I graduated, a little article appeared in the *South China Morning Post,* with the headline "Hong Kong Girl Graduates From Michigan College."

At the time of my graduation, I weighed only 69 pounds, but was the only one of 49 students who had not missed a day of class. I was told that my low weight was a result of all the stress I experienced in high school. I started working as a nurse in the post-operative recovery room at Butterworth Hospital the very day after graduation. It was a great experience, taking care of people who did not realize their need, as they were still asleep from surgery.

After a year of nursing, because my health was still not good, I resigned from Butterworth. I was admitted to the hospital, put on a food pump, and given 48 hours to live. My parents were called to come home from Hong Kong.

Mother arrived first, as Father had to wait to turn over the work in Hong Kong to the Morgans, who were transferring from Japan. When he returned, my father taught missions at Grand Rapids Baptist College. Because of those four years at the college, my father was later able to collect Social Security when my parents retired in Florida. Isn't it amazing how the Lord works?

For the next two years, I took some college courses and worked part time at the Michigan Christian Home. In 1960 I spent five wonderful months with my Uncle Ted and Aunt Edie in England, where I got reacquainted with my father's family.

In 1963, I transferred all of my credits and started full time at

Grand Valley State College (GVSC), majoring in education. At this time, my foster father, John Cederlund, who had been the first superintendent of the Michigan Christian Home for the Aged in Grand Rapids was hospitalized with advanced Parkinson's disease. I moved back with the Cederlunds to help with his care until he passed away in 1966.

During my junior year at GVSC, my whole life began to change. On a Sunday in February 1966, a young man named Jack Miller introduced himself to me. Since he lived alone, he often had supper with my parents and me. My mother was especially taken with him, because they shared a favorite author in C. S. Lewis.

Jack was from Texas. He had been in the U.S. Air Force and, while on leave in New York City, had been led to the Lord by a Christian businessman. Jack moved to Grand Rapids to attend Grace Bible College. Since he lived near Wealthy Street Baptist Church, he attended there.

Jack and I were married on December 17, 1966, at Wealthy Street Baptist Church. At that time I was student teaching, so my whole class attended our wedding.

In June 1967, I graduated with a B.S. in the first class to graduate from Grand Valley State College. Jack and I moved into our first little home. There was lots of remodeling to do in the evenings when Jack came home from work. Then on September 18, 1967, Kathleen Louise Miller, named for Jack's sister, made her appearance. She was such a good baby. Katherine and Grandma Louise Cederlund became instant buddies.

The day after Kathy Lou's birth, Jack enrolled at GVSC. He still had a part of his G.I. Bill, so we managed financially for a while. Then in January of 1968, I started teaching for the Grand Rapids Public Schools. Louise cared for Kathy Lou each day, making it possible for me to teach while Jack attended college. Louise was a great influence on all of us. We thank the Lord for her godly guidance.

Each Saturday morning my father drove over to spend time with his granddaughter. This gave me a chance to give him a haircut when he needed it, or to do my parents' laundry. My father loved to work in the yard and go home with fresh vegetables as much as we looked forward to his weekly visits.

In the spring of 1968, Mr. Hill, superintendent of Kentwood Public Schools where I had been a student teacher, called to tell me I was hired to teach third grade. He gave me three weeks to change my mind. I did not change my mind, and have taught there ever since. I am grateful for the wonderful teaching environment where I work.

In August of 1971, my parents moved to Shell Point Village in Ft. Myers, Florida. Mother felt right at home in the C&MA retirement complex. The Lord gave my parents 20 years of service in Florida. One of the directors said, "We need more people like them here."

When my parents needed extra help during their last four years, Louise Cederlund moved to Florida to care for them. Mother passed away from a heart attack at the age of 88 in 1988. Father had a fatal heart attack at almost 91 in 1991. What a wonderful way to go, awaiting the resurrection day when the Lord comes for His own.

In May of 1972, David Paul Miller completed my small family. Kathy Lou was such a little mother to him. When Jack and I walked in the door with David, Kathy Lou sat in her little rocking chair with a large pillow on her lap. She said, "Right here. I'm all ready!"

In August, we moved into our new home, right across the street from Glenwood Elementary School where I teach. I hoof it each day and get my exercise, which is great—except for icy days. Teaching gets more interesting each year. Maybe I now know more of the "tricks of the trade," skills that are not learned from books. Glenwood Elementary School has an English as a Second Language (ESL) program. In my class of 25 students, nine were born in another country. I think those of us born elsewhere have a greater appreciation for the United States.

In May of 1996, my husband, Jack, had a fatal heart attack at the age of 59. He had been in poor health for 17 years. I believe the words *". . . absent from the body, is present with Lord"* (2 Corinthians 5:8).

t h **i** **r** t y

CHINA REVISITED

My son David, Uncle Jay and Aunt Dorothy Morgan, ABWE's media department staff members Bob Henry and Carl Brandon, and I met in Hong Kong to get organized and to spend Christmas Day with the Lo family. What a reunion! But the most thrilling day, still ahead of us, was December 27, 1985, when we would rejoice with believers in China on the historic occasion of their church building being returned to them after 35 years.

Before departing Hong Kong for Canton, we had a great send-off from ABWE missionaries and Dr. Chung and Dr. Lo (Chee Kwun, my childhood friend), two Chinese doctors now working at the clinic in Hong Kong. I was finally on my way home after 36 years.

We were excited but, naturally, a little apprehensive since few foreigners had visited South China. We were quickly put at ease by the welcoming party waiting for us when we touched down in Canton. Mrs. Dean, wife of an American petroleum engineer, several Chinese Christians, and a few government officials comprised our welcoming committee. I was surprised to find so many people knew we were coming. I was most thrilled to greet Oi Fong, older daughter of Pastor Chen, who thought of me as her baby sister. Her stepmother, Di Goo, had been my *amah* more than 50 years earlier.

There was no privacy for us tourists; we were surrounded everywhere! The most popular member of our group was Carl Brandon, with his "immediate picture camera." Even the stern expressions of the officials melted when they saw themselves in the instant photos.

We walked the Fook Yom Tong (Good Tidings Hall), with the crowds following close on our heels. We had heard that small shops built on the church property were being torn down. Entering the churchyard, we found government tractors still at work removing the rubble. What memories flooded my mind as I entered the church building! It was as if I was a little girl again. Every part of the building triggered vivid memories.

The church building had been turned into government offices, so we were thankful hardly any changes had been made to the physical structure. Everything seemed to be in place except the baptistery, which had been bricked over. The benches, pulpit, and little pump organ were ready for Sunday services. Uncle Jay Morgan said, "Even the nails where we used to hang song scrolls are still here."

The greatest joy was visiting with the believers who could once again meet in their original church building. Word traveled fast, and we were soon in the midst of a joyful reunion with Pastor Chen and his family. It did not take long to recognize my wonderful Chinese family. The Chen children were now grown with families of their own. It was hard to sort out who belonged to whom. Oi Fong came to my rescue by introducing us.

Pastor Chen had saved and trained in the Lui Chau Bible School in the early years of my parents' work. During the period known as the Cultural Revolution, and particularly in the days of the Red Guards, he was beaten, paraded through the streets wearing a dunce cap, and imprisoned. For a while, he, his wife, and their two children were exiled.

Now 90 years old, Pastor Chen had suffered a serious stroke but wore the same sweet smile as always, even though he was confined to a wheelchair. Mrs. Chen, the *amah* who cared for me during my early childhood, kept saying, "My heart is so happy to see my American daughter after so many years."

That first weekend our group went to the old city of Lui Chau, a place in the south that had had no church since the 1930s. The government provided our transportation and an escort wherever we went. We saw signs warning "No foreigners allowed in this area" on the 60-mile journey. Lui Chau is the town where my parents first ministered.

As guests of the district magistrate, the ABWE group and my son and I toured the city's sights, which included the ancient pagoda of Lui Chau and its beautiful gardens. We climbed 190 steps to the top for an incredible view, and walked across a lake on a floating sidewalk. That was quite an experience! We also visited a 1,000-year-old temple that had been turned into a museum, a common trend during the Cultural Revolution. The well in the temple courtyard was still being used after a millenium.

On Sunday the church service included, among the packed crowd, members from the German, French, and American families from the petroleum company in town. How wonderful that we did not need to speak the same language in order to worship the Lord! Government officials, sitting in the front row, filled in their paper work while fulfilling their assigned duty of attending and observing the church service.

The communion service was a glorious witness to our faith. I looked in the faces of all the believers and knew, as Uncle Jay Morgan led the service, our hearts were one—truly in communion with God. It was touching to see Pastor Chen, although feeble, raise his hand to give the benediction. After the communion service, three believers approached Uncle Jay Morgan, stating they wanted to be baptized publicly.

Some traveled many miles to see us, and were especially glad to meet my son, David. I was afraid that I would have difficulty communicating, but amazingly found much of the Chinese language came back to me after more than 30 years.

We heard many unusual stories of God's blessing and protection. One of the deacons, Mr. Yeung, was saved after the Cultural

Revolution. He, like many landowners, had been exiled and sent to Inner Mongolia. It was through this crisis in his life that he accepted Christ as Savior. Then there were the missing faces, such as See Yeun, who was killed because she was a Christian. And my old friend, Titus, had died too. I was the only surviving person of the nine-member youth group of long ago.

We returned to our hotel rooms, exhausted physically and emotionally. My friend Chee Kwun slipped three cans of Campbell's soup and a can opener into my suitcase before I left Hong Kong. She anticipated that we might need them. Did we ever! David and I invited the others to our room for "Sunday dinner." A few crackers and a cup of hot soup sure hit the spot!

My request to visit an elementary school was arranged by the government. A banner of welcome proclaimed the arrival of their American friends. The school had 1,500 students in first through fifth grades, as did 40 other schools in the area. Everywhere we went, smiling little faces watched our every move.

Children in China attend school six days a week from 7:30 a.m. to 5:30 p.m. Each teacher is responsible for 50 students, without an aide to help. The students stand in greeting when their teacher enters the room. Otherwise, they remain seated, reciting their lessons aloud, and speak only when spoken to.

We were invited to tea with the mayor of Ha San (the new name for Fort Bayard). When he heard that my son, David, played table tennis (David won the silver medal for Michigan Junior Olympics in 1985), he arranged matches for David against three men, one of them the school principal. We saw the Lord's hand even in a little ping-pong diplomacy. The men wrote to ask when Di Wie (Cantonese for David) would come back and give them the chance to reverse their defeat.

Another highlight of that week was the arrival of Aunt Sophie Jenista, who with her late husband, Frank, lived in this area for a few months during their first term of missionary work. They worked with my parents and the Morgans in Chek Hom for six months in 1949. Her arrival completed our congenial group of seven.

On Tuesday, a crammed vanload—18 of us—rode to the city of Chek Hom, where I grew up. Chek Hom is now a district of Zhanjiang. I hardly recognized it. I remembered my father's 1935 Chevrolet being the only car to occasionally chug through town. Now cars, buses, bicycles, pedi-cabs, ox carts, and people milled everywhere, with pigs and chickens usually claiming the right-of-way.

It was here, on the temple square (although the temple and huge banyan trees were gone), that Uncle Jay Morgan had been stoned while preaching in 1948. He bore the scars of that incident for the rest of his life. And it was here that Jaymes and I viewed the tiger when it was brought to town and auctioned off, literally, piece by piece. Uncle Jay and Aunt Dorothy experienced an emotional reunion with Mrs. Ma who, along with her late husband, took care of the Morgans' home and belongings when they fled China in 1949.

We walked to the location of my old house. With buildings built side by side, it was hard to distinguish just where the compound would have been. I finally recognized the gnarled old grapevine my father planted 50 years ago; the tile on the porch confirmed that this was my house.

The house was now the local seat of government for Zhanjiang. A five-story building stood in front where the lawn used to be. The doors were locked, and all the workers, dressed in suits, stood a short distance away. While I engaged them in conversation, David went around to each window and took as many pictures of the interior as he could. It was so strange to know that my house had been confiscated by the communists, but I was thankful just to be able to see it.

The Morgans were not allowed to see their old house, as government officials now occupied it. No amount of negotiating could persuade them to let us in the big gates. David did the next-best thing; he and one of Pastor Chen's daughters went up in a tall building across the street and got some good pictures. The day happened to be December 31st, Ann Morgan's birthday.

On New Year's Day, David and I spent some time with Mini, the English interpreter, and her mother, who was a doctor. Five years later, Mini came to live with my family while she attended Cornerstone College in Grand Rapids. Her mother lived in Lui Chow when the Morgans and my family arrived in the Lui Chow market during World War II, and remembers seeing the three white children that day. Mini and her husband, Tom, were even married in our home.

On Thursday, Aunt Sophie Jenista, David, and I went with the vanload of officials and their friends to visit an ancient temple on beautiful Lake Surprise, where my father baptized many believers in the early days of my parents' missionary work. The monks at the temple served us tea in a room I remembered being in as a six-year-old.

On the way home, we offered to take the officials to dinner if they would drive back through my hometown for one last look. So all 18 of us ate dinner on the hotel roof garden I had visited as a child. Well fed and happy, the officials allowed us to walk up Kai Ling (Chicken Hill) and take many priceless pictures.

As the sun was going down, we met again in the church courtyard with the Chen family and took more pictures. So much had happened in the last 36 years, and there were many missing faces. But we know that one day, we will see them again.

That evening we were guests of the mayor for a 20-course dinner, including everything from fish head soup to . . . well . . . you're better off not knowing. But it was all delicious!

Our day of departure arrived all too soon. We said goodbye to our two photographers, Carl Brandon and Bob Henry, as they took a train north to see more of China. David and I walked over to the church to say our last goodbyes. Mrs. Chen, with tears in her eyes, said this was her sixth time saying goodbye to her American baby. I felt the same sadness, as I knew our next reunion would be in heaven. Still, I was grateful to God for allowing me to see these dear friends whose faces had been dimmed in childhood memories.

I waved from the plane window, watching the Chinese landscape drop away. I wondered if I would ever see any of those people again. Yet my heart was quiet with the knowledge that my friends rest safely in the hands of our sovereign God. And while I may never return to this wonderful, exotic place that was my home and still holds a special place in my heart, I draw a great sense of satisfaction from knowing that I will see many of those long-ago friends when I reach my heavenly Home. What a reunion that will be! We'll have all of eternity to spend together in the presence of our Savior, the One for whom my parents went to China in the first place.

I can look back on all these years and see a pattern, not of perfection, but of deliberate Christ-likeness.

Eventually, both of our children married. Kathy married Kurt VanderWeide, and they have two sons, Andrew and James. Kathy uses her teaching skills as a home-schooling mom. One Thursday a month, she and the boys go to Wealthy Park Baptist Church to work on missionary projects.

David married Tina Robertson in June of 1999. They live in Chattanooga, Tennessee, where David is dean of men at Tennessee Temple University. Tina teaches sign language in a public school.

On September 3, 1999, a heart attack took our beloved Grandma Louise Cederlund to be with the Lord. She was almost 93 and had been alert right to the end. She lived with me for the last 11 years of her life. We all miss her.

I am often asked, "When will you retire?" Dr. Mary Leiker, my superintendent, says, "Take your vitamins, and you'll be good for another 20 years." Although teaching gets better each year, I find myself longing for the warmer climate of my childhood. I'll relocate to Tennessee one of these days, to live with David and Tina.

Truly I am blessed of the Lord to have had such a rich life. My parents were people of prayer, always consulting the Lord for guidance, no matter what they did. They passed along a great heritage. I am so thankful that my children and grandchildren are walking in the ways of the Lord.

EPILOGUE

My grade school years were "seasoned" with many of my mother's stories now preserved in this book. Seasoned, I say, because I heard the history, often after meals. It enhanced my understanding of God through her consistent acknowledgment that God had provided for and protected her, my grandparents (Victor and Margaret Barnett), and the Morgans as they served Him.

Here is food for thought: the same God who cares about missionaries in China cares about you. He cares about all the details of your life, and He cares about whether or not you will spend eternity with Him, because He loves you.

God wants an eternal personal relationship with you, but there is a problem. The Bible says, *"All have sinned."* Our sin makes a personal relationship with God impossible, because He is holy, without sin. The Bible also says that there is a price for sin: *"The wages of sin is death."* Each of us must pay the punishment for sin, which would keep us away from God forever.

There is, however, really Good News! *"The wages of sin is death, but the gift of God is eternal life through Jesus Christ our Lord"* (Romans 6:23). *"For God so loved the world, that He gave His only begotten Son, that whosoever believeth in Him should not perish* [have to pay for his/her own sin] *but have everlasting life"* (John 3:16). *"If thou shalt confess with the mouth the Lord Jesus, and shall believe in thine heart that God hath raised Him from the dead, thou shalt be saved"* (Romans 10:9).

Is Jesus, the Son of God, your personal Savior? It doesn't matter how many times you've attended church, how much good you have achieved, or who your ancestors are. What is important is that your sin was paid for by Jesus Christ. God loved you so much that He sent His own Son as your substitute so that you can have an eternal relationship with Him beginning right now. If you would like to be saved, simply agree with God that you are a sinner and cannot save yourself from punishment. Ask Jesus to be your Savior. Tell Him that you believe God raised him from the grave in order to complete your payment. And then thank Him for your salvation.

Salvation is God's free gift of His son, Jesus. Putting your faith in Him saves you from eternal punishment for sin, and enables you to have an eternal relationship with God, the kind of relationship revealed in this book.

David Miller
May 2001